GIFTED & TALENTED™

Reading, Writing & Math

Cover Illustration by Mark Stephens
Written by Tracy Masonis and Larry Martinek, Math Consultant

Spark Publishing

Dear Parents,

Gifted & Talented Reading, Writing & Math has been designed specifically to promote development of analytic thinking, language arts, and math skills. The activities in this book use a variety of critical strategies, including activities to spark your child's imagination, encourage brainstorming, and sharpen math skills.

The activities are intended to help develop reading, writing, and math skills that your child will use at school and home. Most of the activities can be completed directly on the workbook pages. In some instances, though, your child might like to use a separate sheet of paper to interpret what has been read or work out math problems.

While working in this book, your child may be inspired to create his or her own story or math problems. If so, have your child present his or her work and explain the strategies to you. Praise your child's efforts, and encourage him or her to continue creating them. This type of activity not only stimulates creativity and independent thinking, but also deepens your child's love of learning.

Adapted from *Gifted & Talented® Reading, Writing & Math Grade PreK*

Spark Publishing
A Division of Barnes & Noble
120 Fifth Avenue
New York, NY 10011
www.sparknotes.com

ISBN-13: 978-1-4114-0321-5
ISBN-10: 1-4114-0321-5

For more information, please visit *www.flashkidsbooks.com*
Please submit changes or report errors to *www.flashkidsbooks.com/errors*

Printed and bound in Canada

15 14 13 12 11 10
12/14

Table of Contents—Reading

Groups/Classification

Sequencing

Context Clues

Making Inferences

Predicting Outcomes

Table of Contents—Writing

Print Awareness/Core Sight Words for Writing and Reading

Vocabulary/Labeling

Graphic Organizers for Pre-Writing/Writing

Table of Contents—Math

Numbers and Operations

Patterns

Geometry and Spatial Sense

Measurement

Classification and Data Collection

Number Concepts

Name

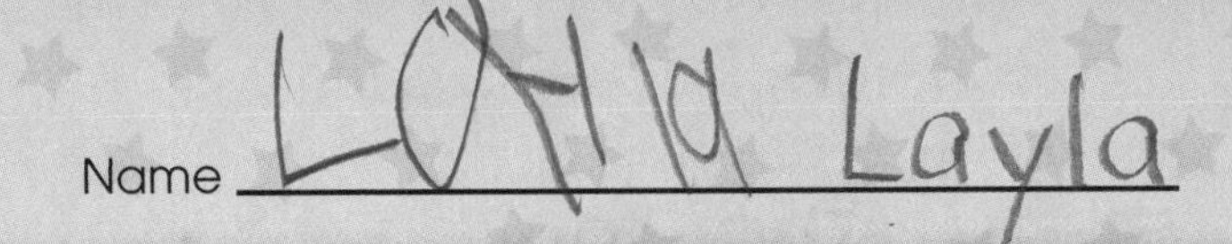

Frank's Fish Tank

Look at Frank's new fish tank.
Can you find the biggest fish?
How many fish are red?
Which fish is the tiniest?
Which fish is wearing glasses?
Which fish is the skinniest?

How many fish are there altogether in the fish tank?

Draw a big check mark on your favorite fish.

The Zoo

Name Laila

Many animals live in the zoo. Find the animals that are small. Which animals are large? Which animals do you think eat a lot? Which animals are soft?

Which animal would you want for a pet? Why?

Circle your favorite animal above.

Name Lotia

Tom, Tinkerbell, and Tulip

Tom is a large cat. His sister Tinkerbell is a very small cat. They have another sister named Tulip, who is a medium-sized cat.

In the space between Tom and Tinkerbell, draw a picture of Tulip.

Name

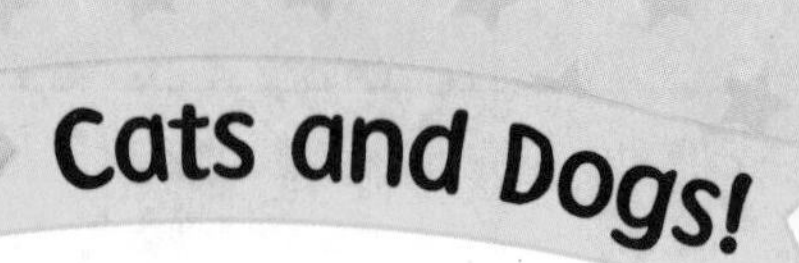

Look at the cat and dog below.
Can you name two ways that they are the same?
Can you name two ways that they are different?

What would you name the cat?
What would you name the dog?
Which do you like better, the cat or the dog?

 Draw a big check mark on your choice.

Name L9414

Pam's Purple Shoes!

Pam loves to wear purple shoes. All her shoes are purple! Draw a line connecting each pair of matching shoes.

Which pair of shoes should Pam wear to the beach?
Which pair of shoes should she wear with her pajamas?

Circle your favorite pair of shoes above.

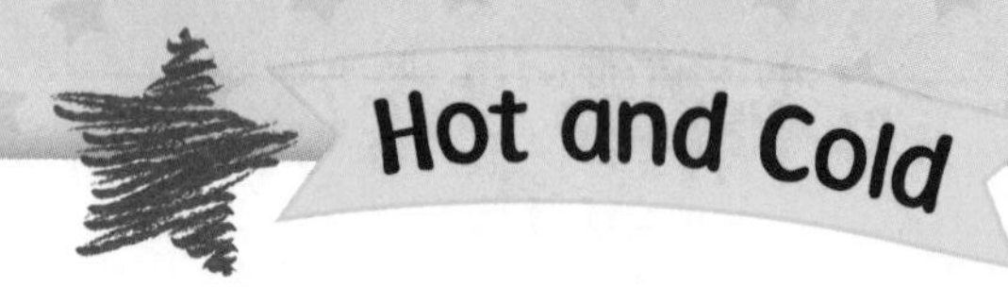

Hot and Cold

Name 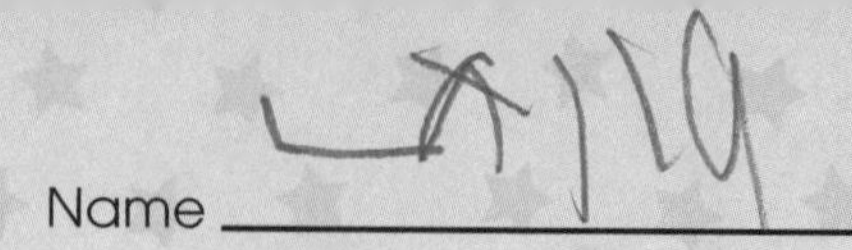

Miriam's mom just made breakfast. What things are hot on the table? What things are cold?

 Circle all the hot things with a red crayon.

 Circle all the cold things with a blue crayon.

What would you eat for breakfast if you were Miriam?

Name ______________________

Fast and Slow

Look at the picture below.

Draw a circle around all the things that go fast.

X Draw an **X** on each thing that goes slow.

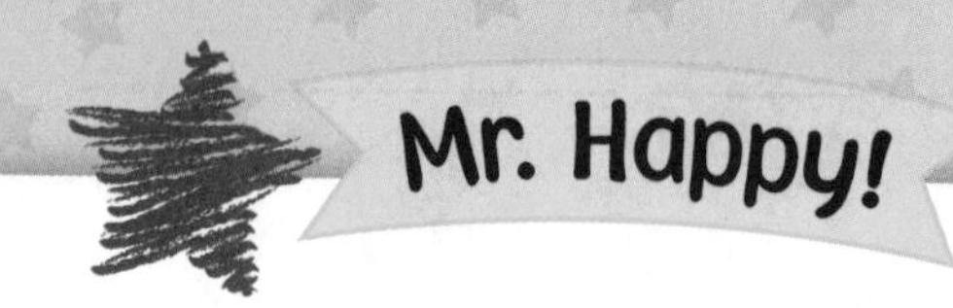

Mr. Happy!

Name ____________________

Mr. Happy sells only food that is orange or yellow! What things are yellow? What things are orange?

Oh, no! The food in Mr. Happy's picnic basket has lost its color! Color the food using colors that make sense.

Name ______________________________

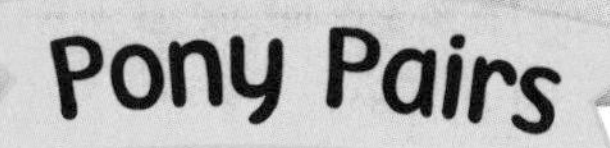

Pony Pairs

Each pony in the field has a twin! Draw a line to connect the twins.

How many ponies are there altogether?

Circle the pony that is your favorite color.
Would you like to ride a pony?

Name ______________________

A baby bear is called a cub. Each cub looks like its mother.

Draw a line to match each cub to its mama bear.

Did you know that bears hibernate in the winter?
What color are the bears that are sleeping?
What is a baby bear called?
Are you a cub?

Name ______________________

Look at this fish! His name is Fish Face.

Only 1 fish below is exactly like Fish Face. Draw a circle around it. What is different about each of the other fish?

Name ______________________________

Lollipop, Lollipop!

There are lots of lollipops in the candy store. In each row below, circle the lollipop that is the same as the one in the jar at the beginning of the row.

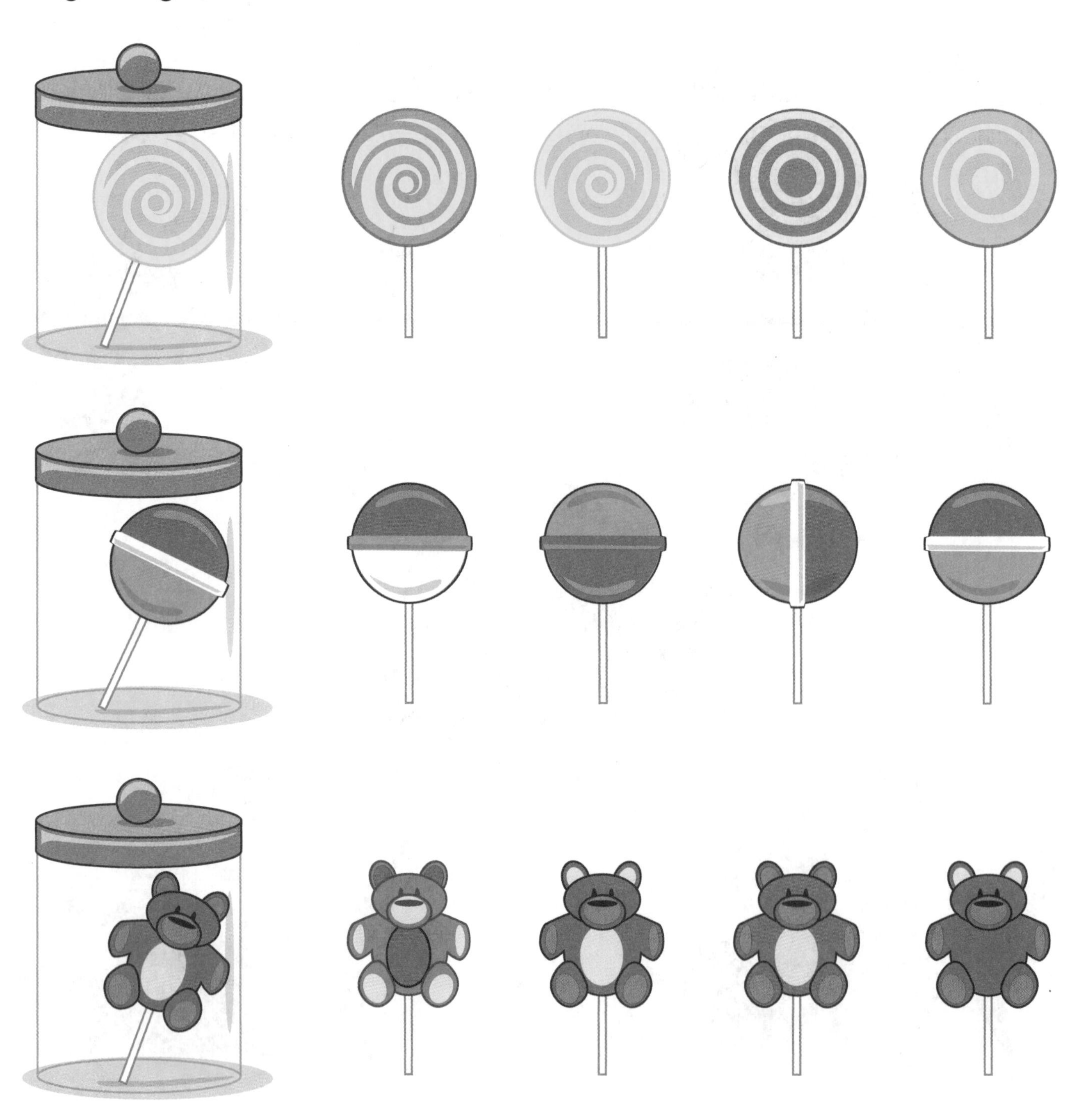

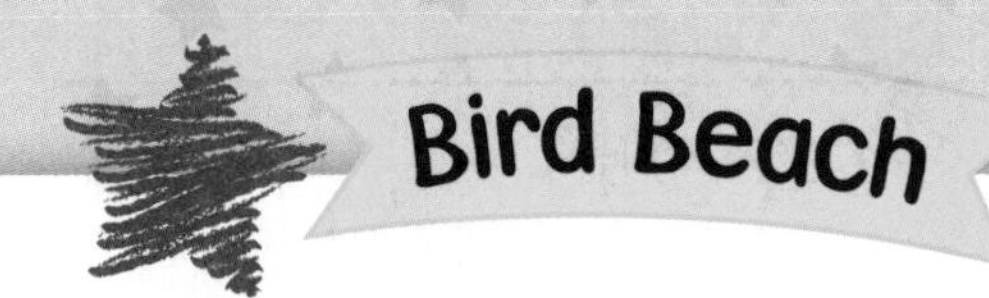

Bird Beach

Name ____________________

There is a beach just for birds. It is called Bird Beach. All the birds like to go there.

Which bird is on something soft? Color that bird pink.
Which bird is on something hard? Color that bird gray.

Which bird is wet? Color that bird green.
Which bird is dry? Color that bird yellow.

Which bird is hot? Color that bird red.
Which bird is cold? Color that bird blue.

Name L

Opposites!

Look at the pictures below. Draw a line to match each picture to its opposite.

Name ____________________

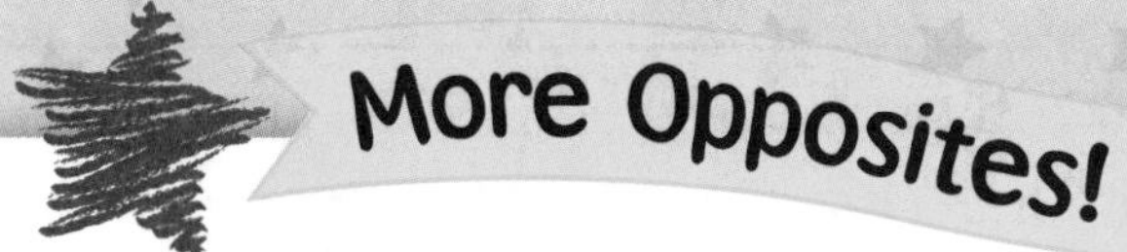

Look at the pictures below. Draw a line to match each picture to its opposite.

Name ____________________

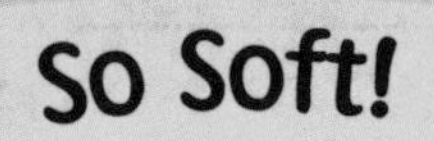

So Soft!

Which objects below are soft? Color all the soft things yellow. Color the rest of the objects using your favorite colors.

Iggy and Piggy

Name ___________________________

Iggy the iguana and Piggy the piglet got lost at the airport. Help them find their families.

Use a green crayon to draw a line to connect everyone in Iggy's family together. Use a pink crayon to connect everyone in Piggy's family together.

Name ___________________________

Part of a Group

Pick 3 pictures that go together in each group. Draw an **X** on the picture that does **not** belong in the group.

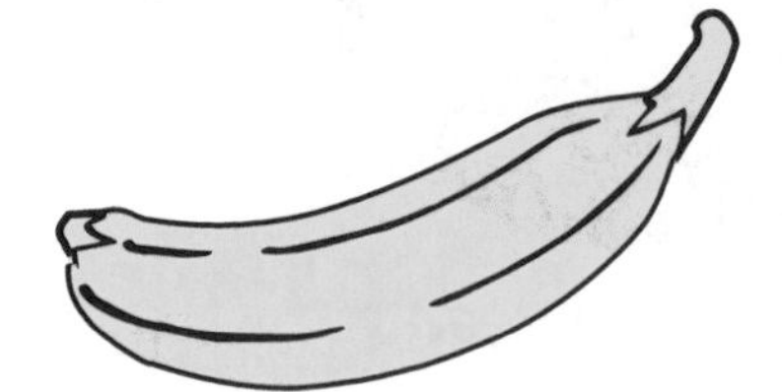

Name ____________________

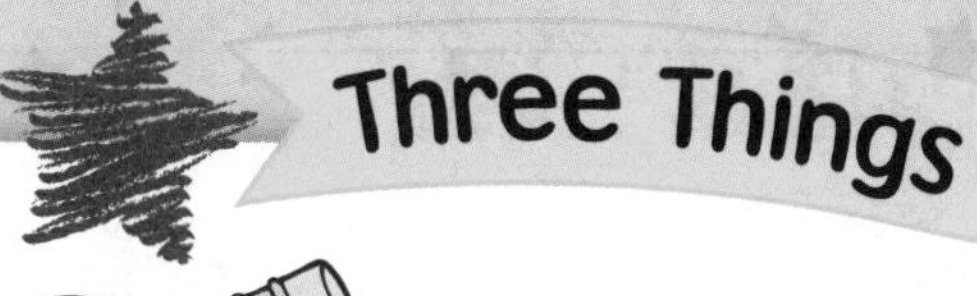

Three Things

Circle your answers below.

Which 3 things are on your face?

 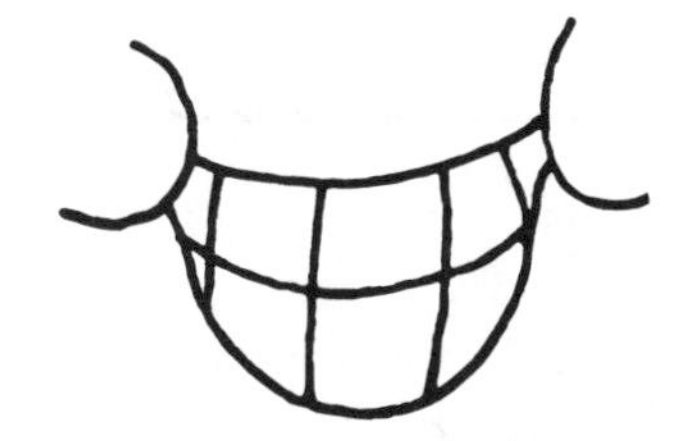 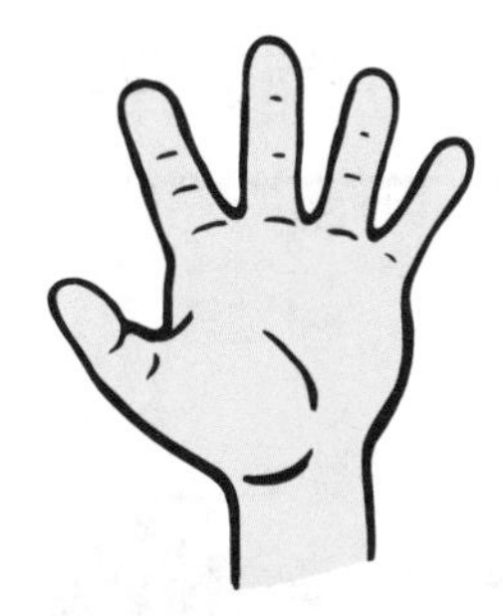 

Which 3 things would you need to sleep?

Which 3 animals like to go in the water?

Which 3 things would you wear if you were cold?

Name ____________________

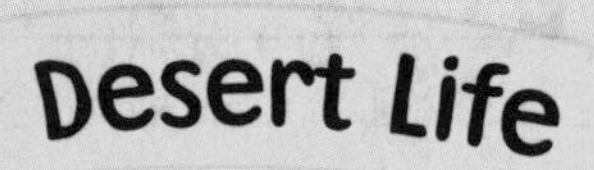

Desert Life

Many different kinds of animals live in the desert. Some of the animals pictured below belong in the desert and some do not. Which animals do not belong? Draw an **X** on each picture that does **not** belong in the group.

Name ____________________

Chelsea's Cupcakes!

Chelsea and her dad made cupcakes for her mom's birthday. They put them on a plate. Two cupcakes do not belong. Circle the 2 cupcakes that do **not** belong.

Name ___________________________

Wrong Blue Things

There are lots of blue things in the picture below. But some of them are not supposed to be blue! Circle 5 things that should **not** be blue.

Name ____________________

What Does Not Belong?

In each row below, use the clue to find the answer. Circle the 1 picture that does **not** begin with the letter **M**.

Circle the 1 picture that does **not** begin with the letter **D**.

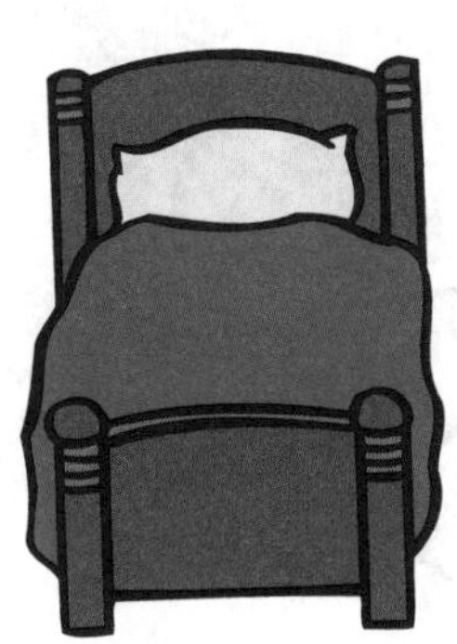

Circle the 1 picture that does **not** begin with the letter **F**.

Look at the pictures that you circled. Make up a story about them. On a separate sheet of paper, draw a picture to go with your story.

Name ______________________________

Tricky Teddy Bears!

Choose 1 of the teddy bears, and explain why it does not belong with the others. Then choose another teddy bear, and find a new reason why it does not belong with the other teddy bears.

Name ______________________________

Line Up, Mr. Rabbit!

These rabbits were told to line up in order from biggest to smallest. But something is wrong. The rabbit that should be first is not where he belongs! Find the rabbit that is out of order and circle it.

Name ______________________________

Jack's Brothers

There are 7 boys in Jack's family. Each brother is a little bit taller than the next brother.

 Who is the tallest brother?

 Who is the shortest brother?

 Who is in the middle?

How tall do you want to be?

Name ______________________________

Michael the Monkey

Michael the Monkey needs help getting dressed. Can you help him? Point to what he should he put on first. What should he put on second? What should he put on third? Then circle the last thing he should put on.

Name ____________________

Ruff! Ruff!

Finish the drawing below. Use a pencil or a crayon to connect the dots in order. Can you guess what it is? Start at 1 and end at 10.

Name ____________________

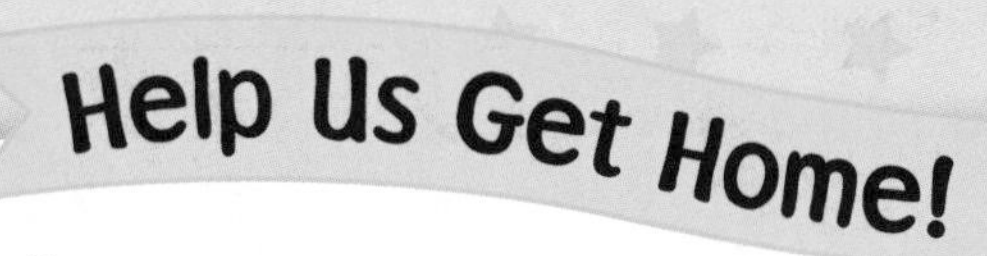

Help Us Get Home!

Help each animal get home! Use your finger to trace a path from left to right. Then draw a line with a pencil or a crayon to connect each animal with its home.

Name ______________________________

Follow, Follow!

Follow the animals with your finger as they move across the page. Then draw a line with a pencil or a crayon to trace each path.

Name ____________________

Color Those Cows!

Color the cows using the clues below.

The brown cow is hiding.
The black and pink spotted cow is eating.
The blue cow is fat!

Name ___________________________

Stop Making Sense!

Look at the picture. A lot of silly things are happening! Circle all of the things that do **not** make sense.

Rainbow Clues

Follow the clues below to circle your answers.

Circle the object that is red and **soft**.

Circle the object that is orange and **small**.

Circle the object that is yellow and **sweet**.

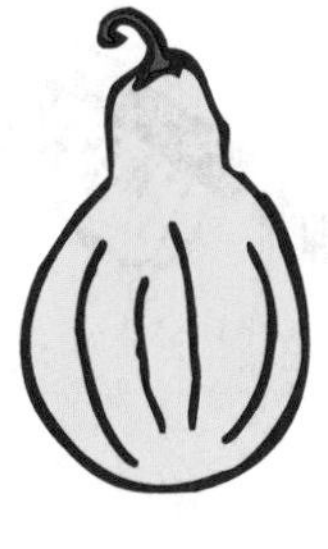
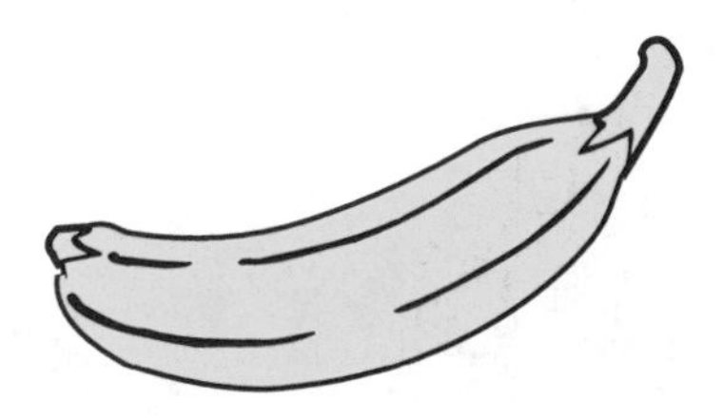

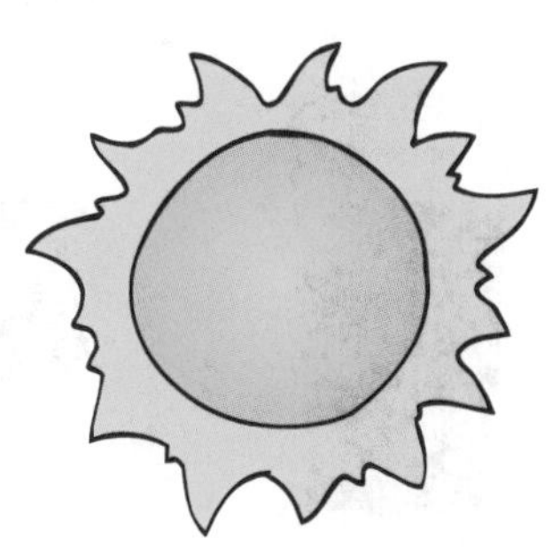

Circle the object that is green and **long**.

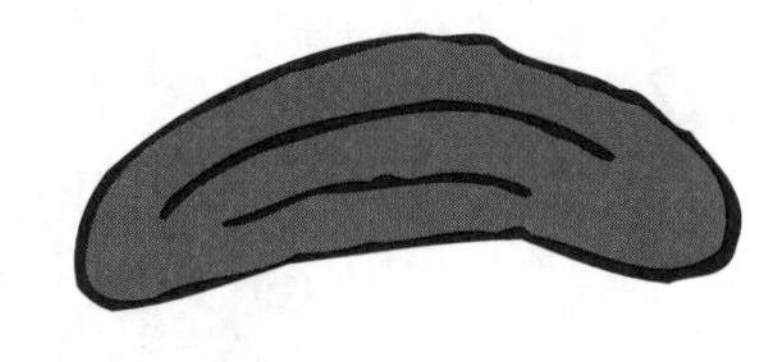

Name ____________________

More Rainbow Clues

Follow the clues below to circle your answers.

Circle the object that is blue and **sweet**.

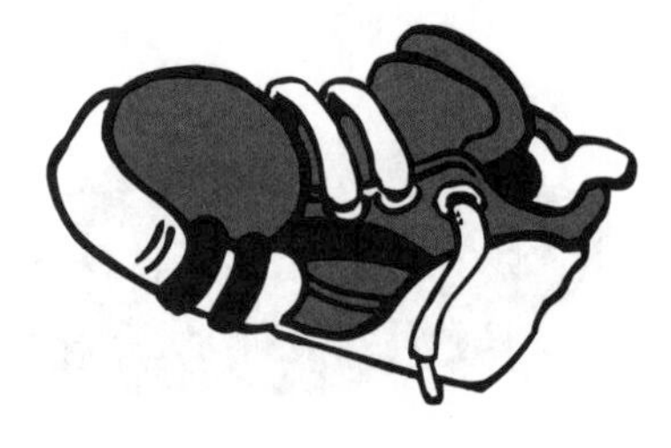

Circle the object that is purple and **furry**.

Circle the object that is brown and **chewy**.

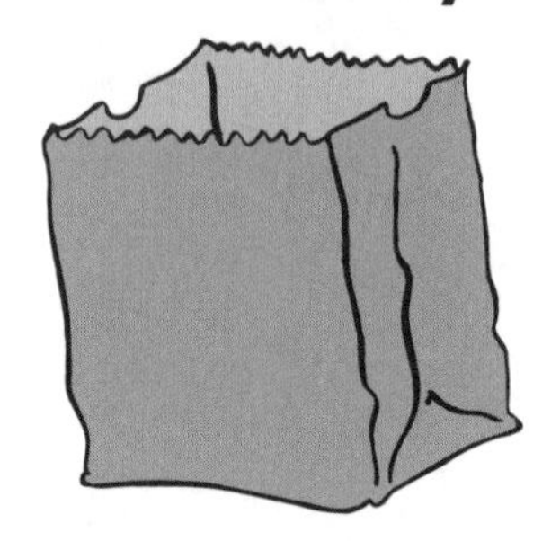
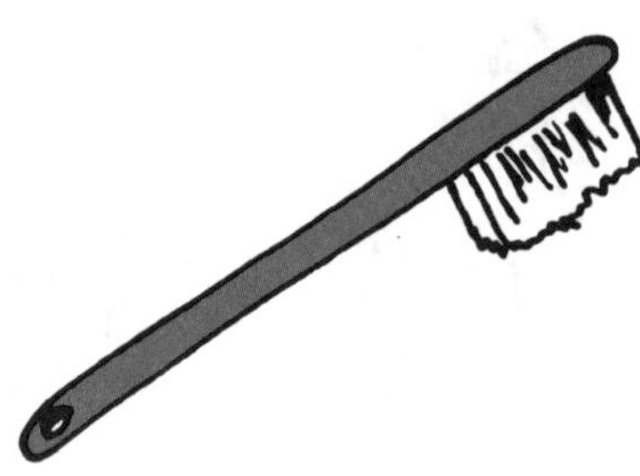

Circle the object that is **black** and **large**.

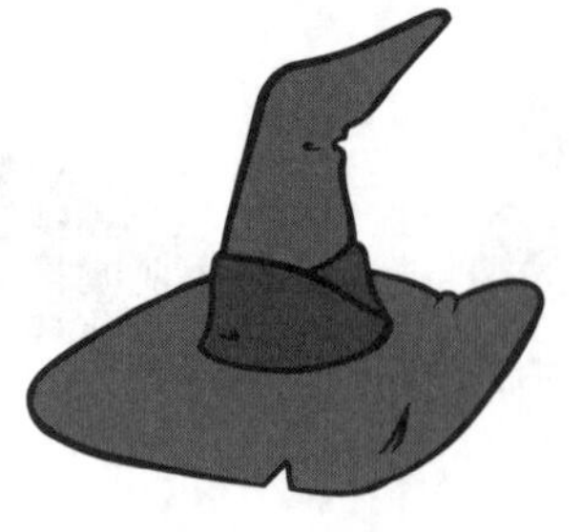

Color It In!

Name ___________________________

Color the 1 picture in each row that both words describe.

soft and **cold**

   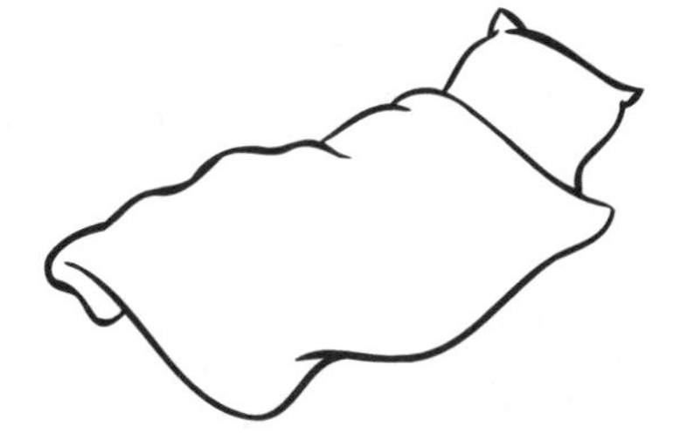

tall and **large**

hot and **round**

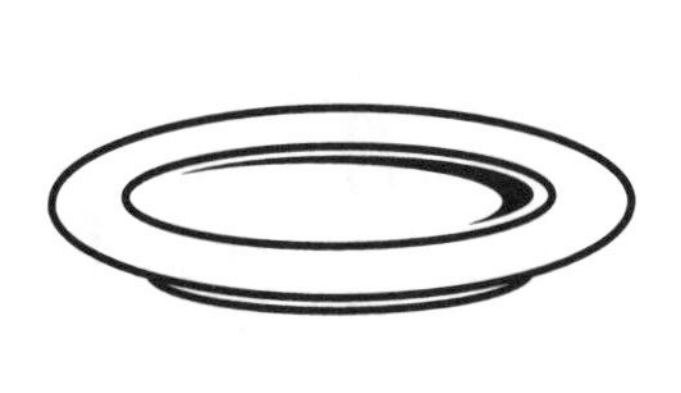   

shiny and **hard**

   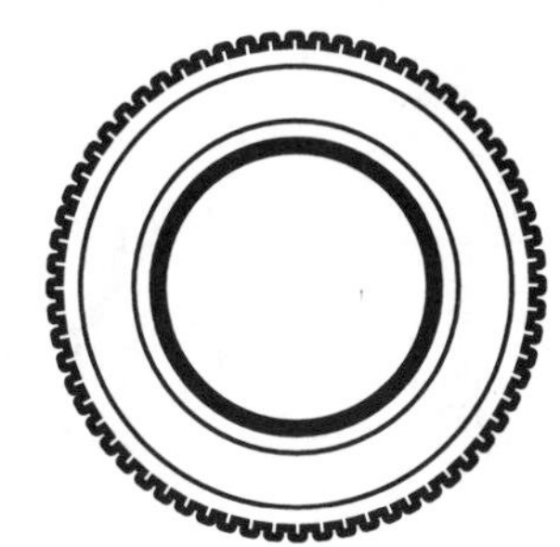

Color It In Again!

Name ____________________

Color the 1 picture in each row that both words describe.

square and **hard**

sticky and **pink**

smooth and **cold**

wet and **large**

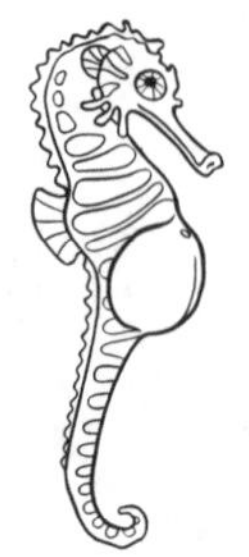

Name ______________________________

Pink Riddles

Find the picture that answers each riddle and color it pink. Color the other pictures in a way that makes sense.

I am pink and sweet. I am also fluffy. What am I?

I am pink and soft. I also have feathers. What am I?

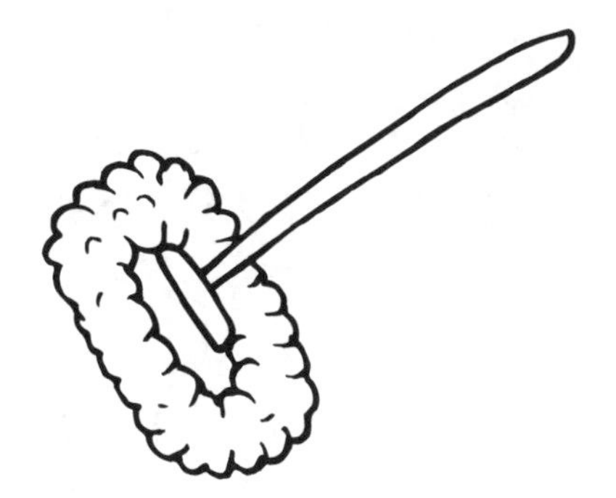

I am pink and small. I smell pretty. What am I?

Name ____________________

Ben's New Sister!

Ben is going to see his new baby sister for the first time! Ben and his dad are at the hospital looking at all the sleeping babies. Use the clues to find out which baby is Ben's new sister. Then circle your choice.

Ben's sister is not bald.
Ben's sister has a yellow blanket.
Ben's sister has dark hair.

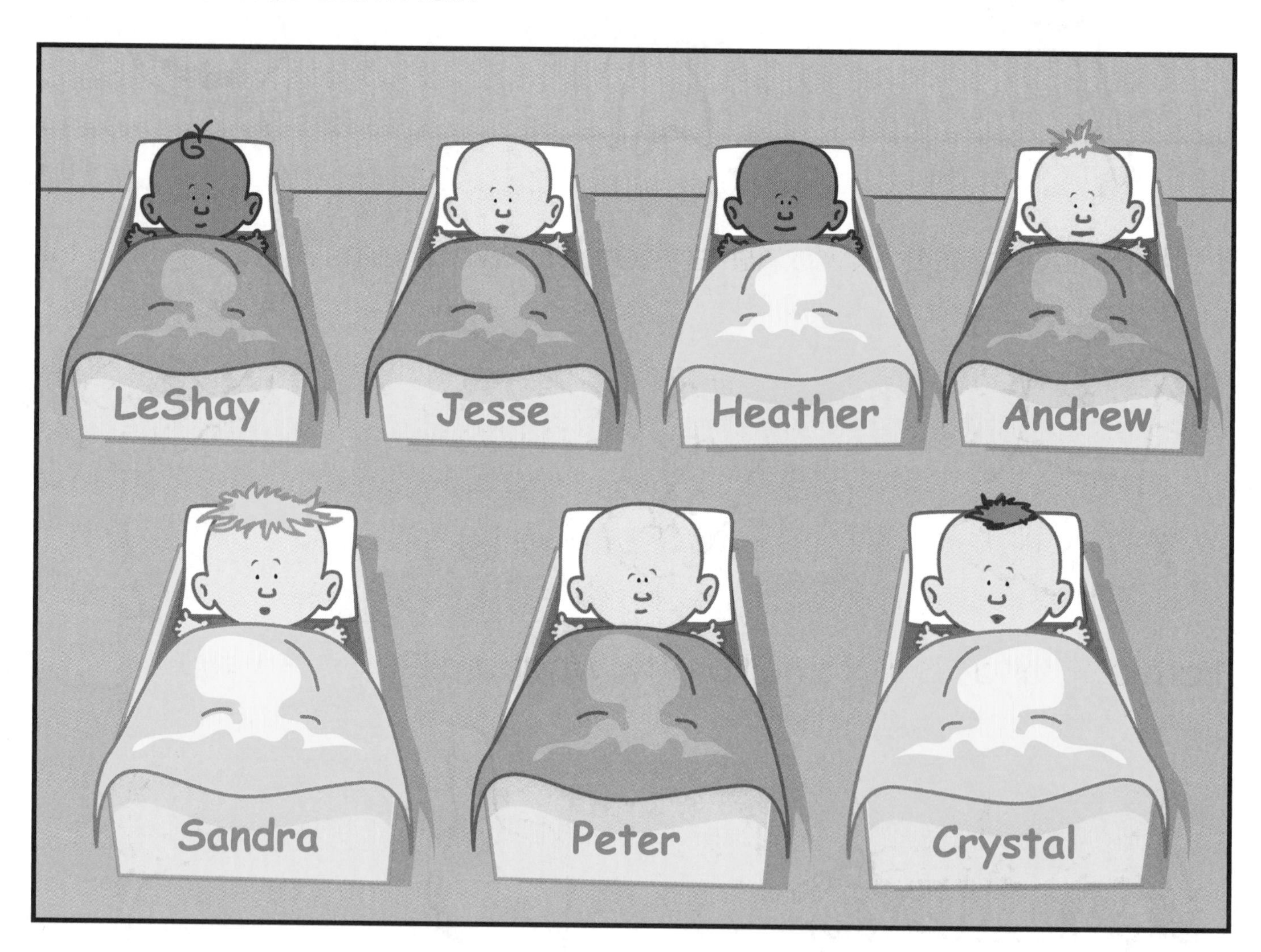

What is Ben's sister's name?

Name ___________________________

Tim's Turtle

Help Tim pick out a turtle at the pet shop.

Tim does **not** want a turtle with circles on its back.
Tim does **not** want a green turtle.
Tim does **not** want a turtle with triangles on its back.

Circle the turtle that Tim should pick.

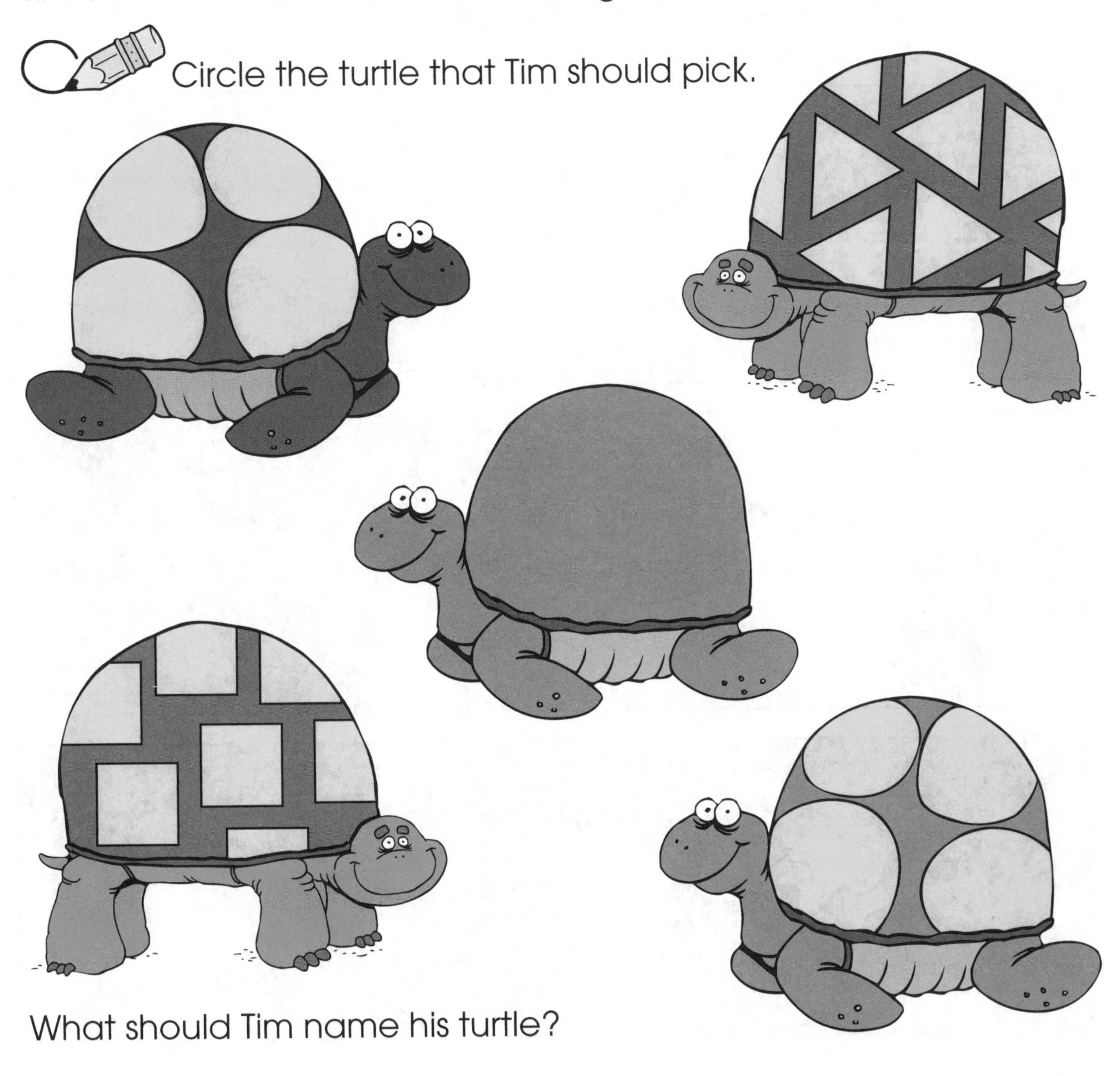

What should Tim name his turtle?

Name ____________________

Find the Right Picture

Which picture goes with the sentence? Draw a big check mark on the correct picture.

The 3 little pigs had a picnic in the tree to escape from the big bad wolf.

Name ________________

Which picture goes with the sentence? Draw a big check mark on the correct picture.

Marilyn and Mindy went on a Ferris wheel ride with their parents.

Name ______________________________

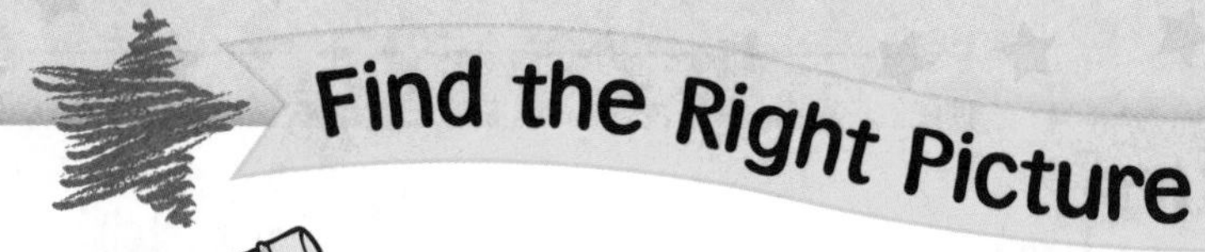

Find the Right Picture

Which picture goes with the sentence? Draw a big check mark on the correct picture.

Raju and her mom spent Saturday alone.
They painted pictures together.

Name ____________________

Which Picture Is Missing?

Look at the pictures on this page. Look at them carefully. Now turn the page.

Name ______________________________

Which Picture Is Missing?

One piece of fruit has been eaten. Draw and color a picture of the missing piece of fruit.

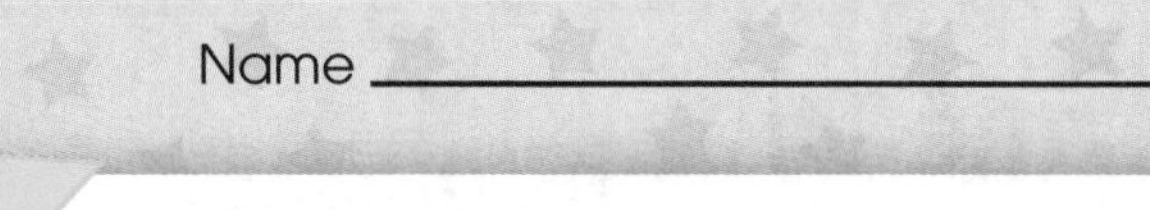

Look at the pictures on this page. Look at them carefully. Now turn the page.

Name ____________________

The Missing Donut!

One donut is missing! Somebody ate it! Draw and color a picture of the missing donut.

Name ______________________________

Which Picture Is Missing?

Look at the pictures below. There is a picture missing.

Draw a big check mark on which one is the missing picture.

Name ______________________

Which Picture Is Missing?

Look at the pictures below. There is a picture missing.

 Draw a big check mark on which one is the missing picture.

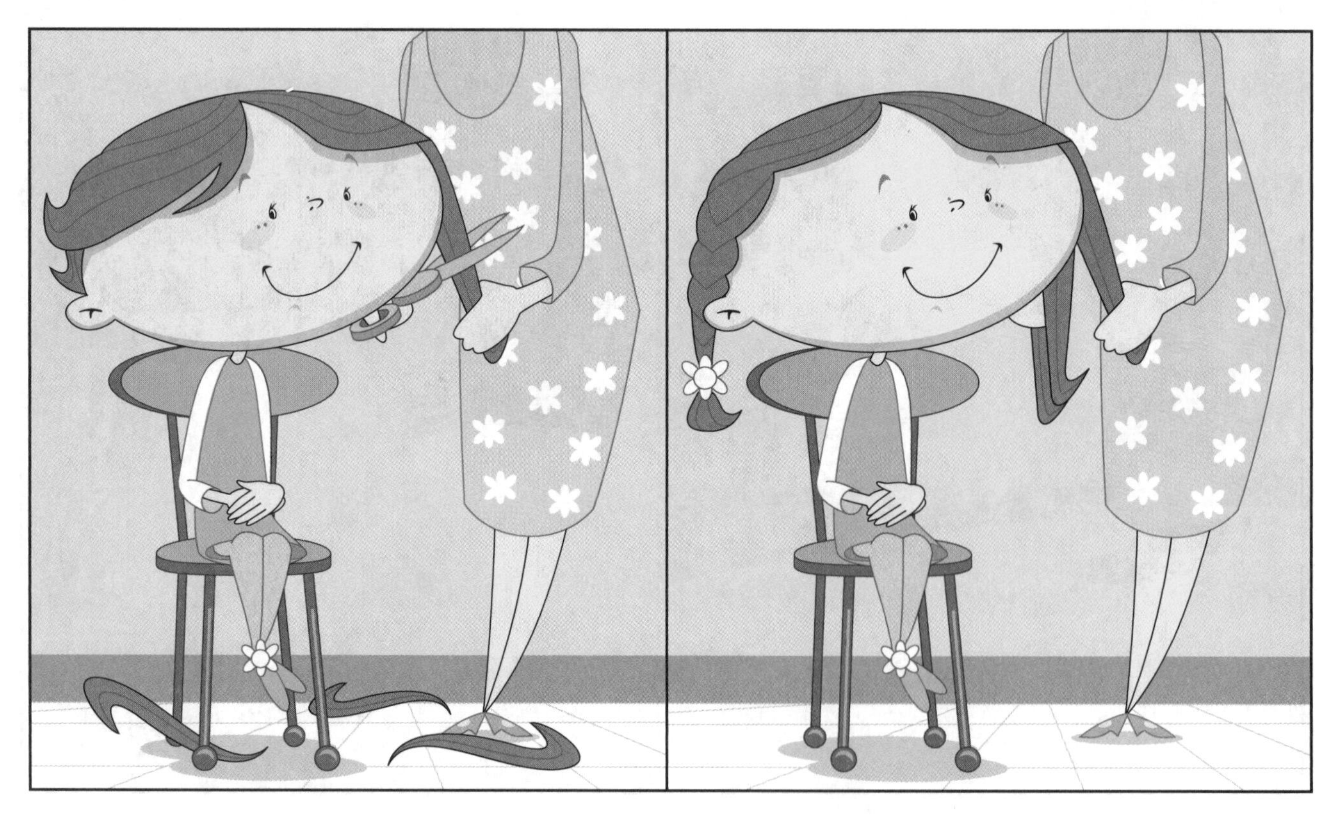

Name ____________________

Which Picture Is Missing?

Look at the pictures below. There is a picture missing.

Draw a big check mark on which one is the missing picture.

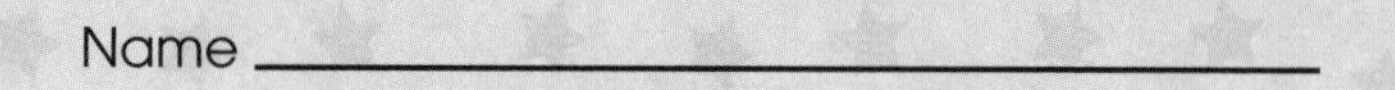

I'm Hungry!

Name ____________________

Draw a line to match each animal to the food it likes to eat.

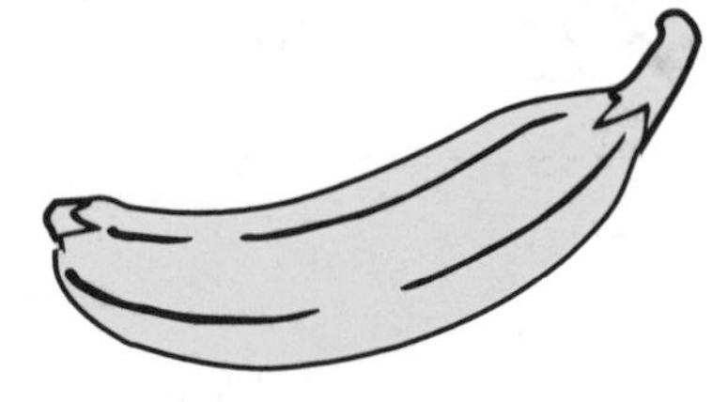

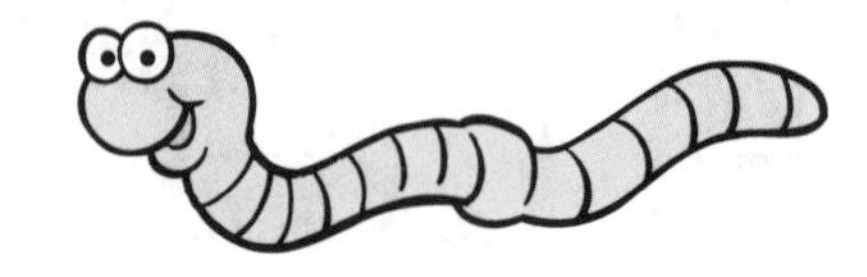

Not in the Nest!

Name 

A mother robin wants to build a nest for her new babies.

Draw an **X** on the things she will not need.

Then draw a picture of some other things she might need.

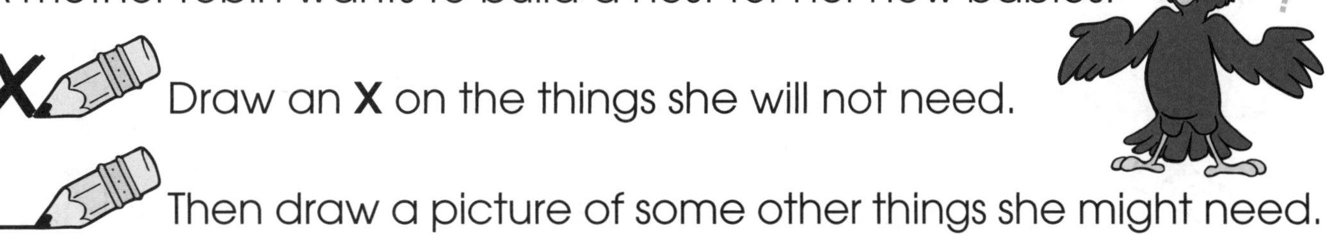

Name ______________________________

Marcy and her dad want to build a doghouse for their new puppy.

Draw an **X** on the things they do not need.

Then draw pictures of some other things they might need.

Name ___________________________

Super Ice-Cream Sundaes!

Janet and her mom want to make ice-cream sundaes.

 Draw an **X** on the things they do not need.

 Then draw pictures of some other things they might need.

Name ______________________________

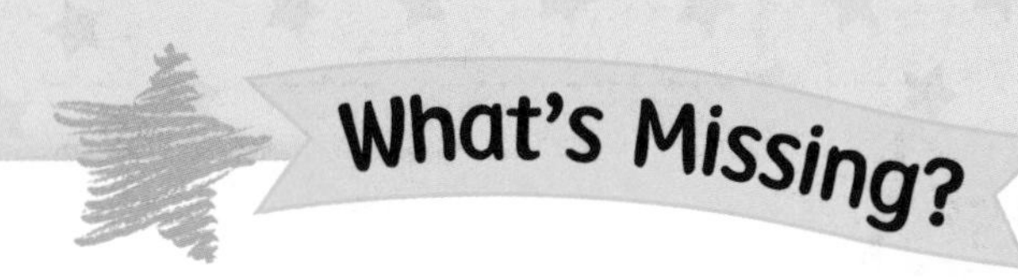

What's Missing?

Look at the pictures below. They start to make a story. The last box is empty.

Which of these pictures helps finish the story? Draw a circle around it.

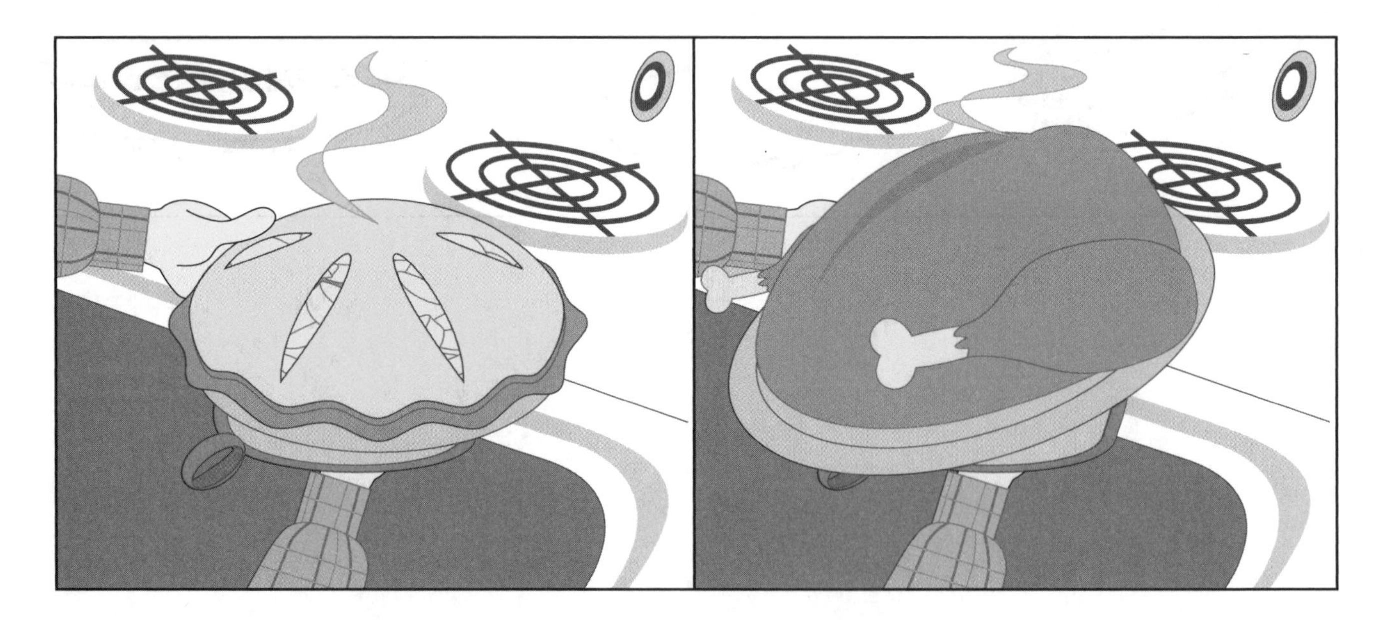

What is your favorite dessert?

Name ______________________________

Look at the pictures below. They start to make a story. The last box is empty.

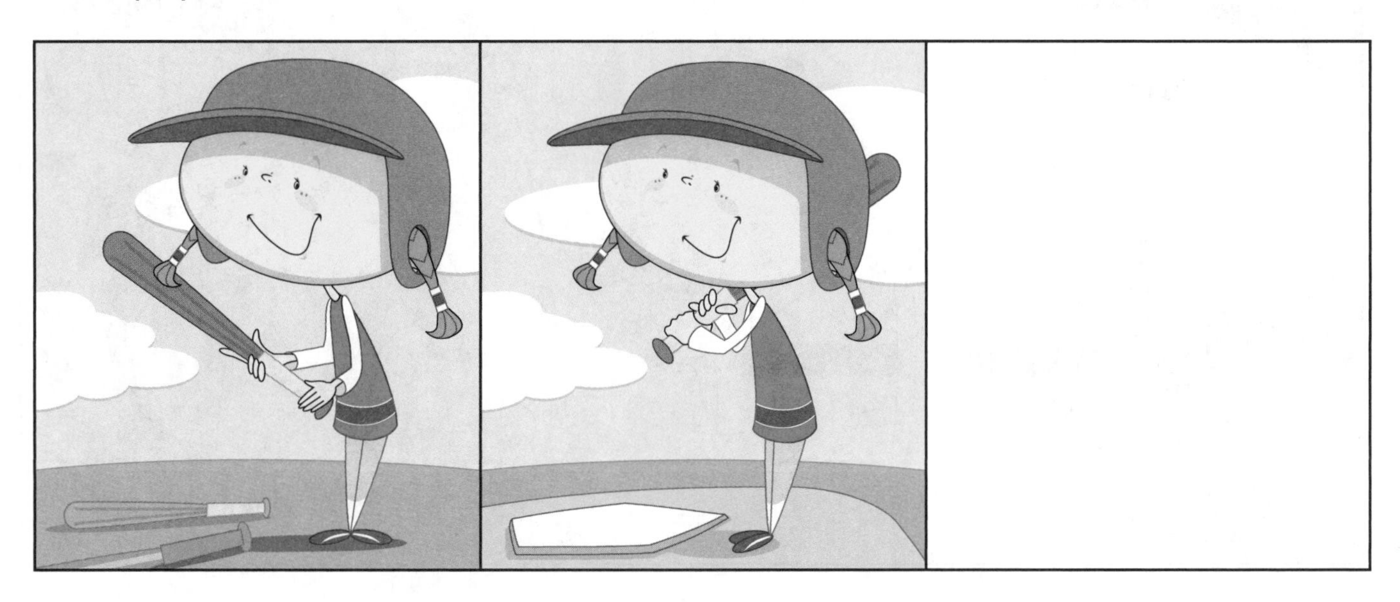

Which of these pictures helps finish the story? Draw a circle around it.

Name ____________________

What Will Happen Next?

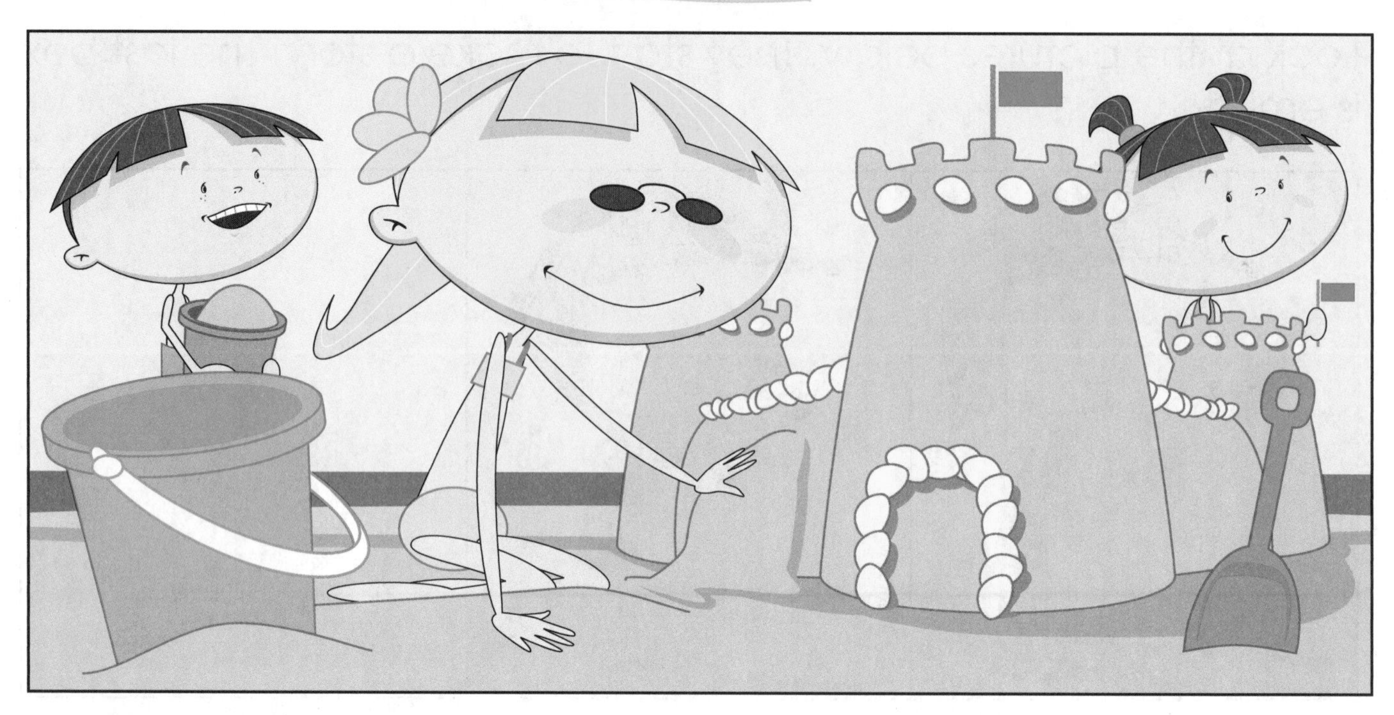

Look at the picture above.

Now circle the picture below that shows what happens next.

Name ____________________

What Will Happen Next?

Look at the picture above.

Now circle the picture below that shows what happens next.

Name ______________________________

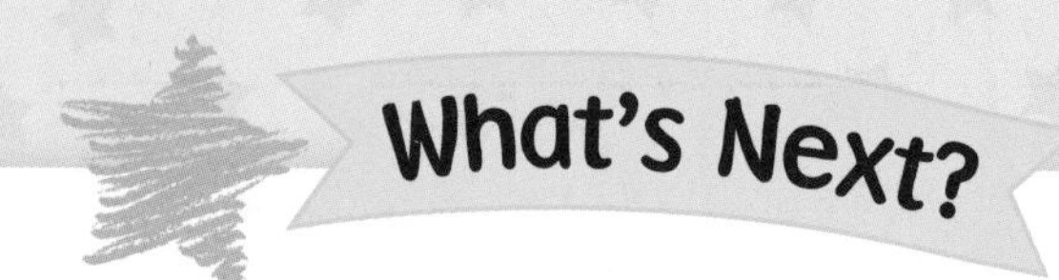

Look at the picture above.

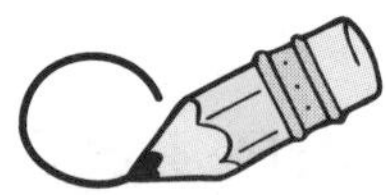

Now circle the picture below that shows what happens next.

Name ______________________________

Letters of the Alphabet

These are the letters of the alphabet. Each letter has a big size and a small size. Say each letter aloud.

The name of each picture begins with the sound of the letters below it. Say the name of the picture aloud, too.

Oops! A few pictures are missing over the letters. If you come to a letter without a picture, then name something that starts with that letter.

More Letters of the Alphabet

These are the rest of the letters of the alphabet. Each letter has a big size and a small size. Say each letter aloud.

The name of each picture begins with the sound of the letters below it. Say the name of the picture aloud, too.

Oops! A few pictures are missing over the letters. If you come to a letter without a picture, then name something that starts with that letter.

Name ______________________

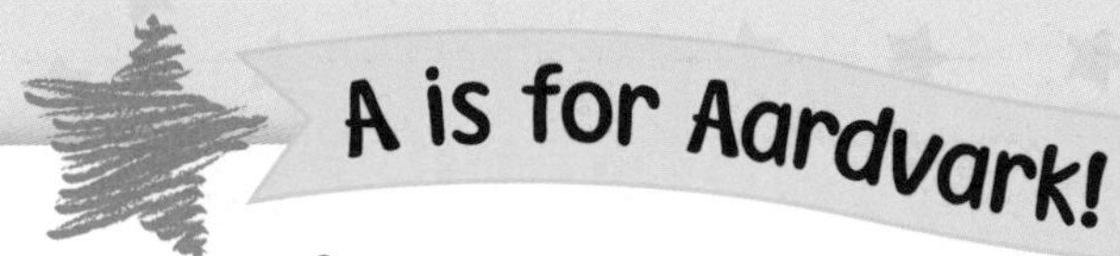

Trace the outline of the letter **A** and **a** below.

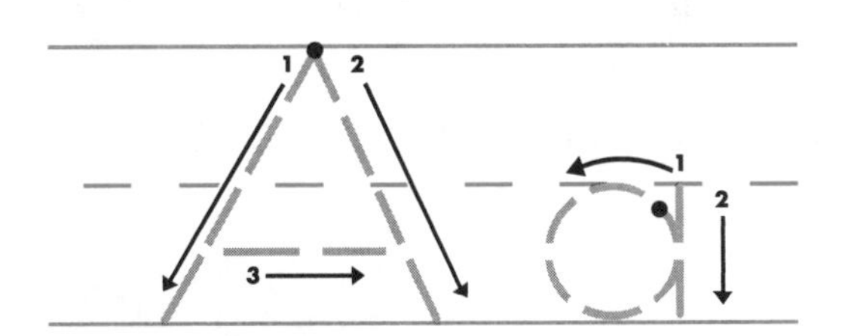

Here are three words that start with **A** or **a**. Trace the dotted **A** and **a** on the words, and then say them aloud.

A	**A** cat was sleeping.	
and	Tom **and** Mom are happy.	 and
away	The balloon flew **away**.	away

Name ______________________________

All Those A's!

Look at the words below that start with **A** or **a**. Say them aloud.

All
am
Are
at
Ate

Read the story below and circle all the words that start with **A** or **a**!

"I am hungry!" said Cat.
"Are we going to eat soon?"

Cat's mom said, "We ate at 12 o'clock, and you ate all of the food! Are you *still* hungry?"

"Yes, I am!" said Cat smiling.

Name ____________________

Begins With B

Trace the outline of the letter **B** and **b** below.

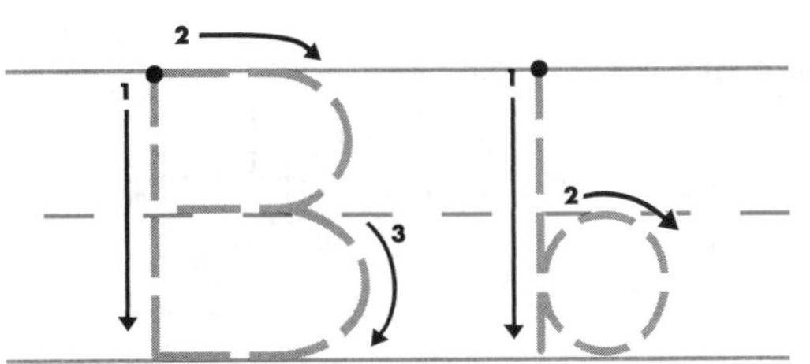

Here are some words that start with **B** or **b**. Say them aloud, and then color the big, silly monster blue.

big
blue
Boo

The big blue monster also has a **black** and **brown** brother. They like to say "Boo!" Color them in **black** and **brown**. Then say the words aloud.

Name ______________________________

Can Carmen Come Over?

Trace the outline of the letter **C** and **c** below.

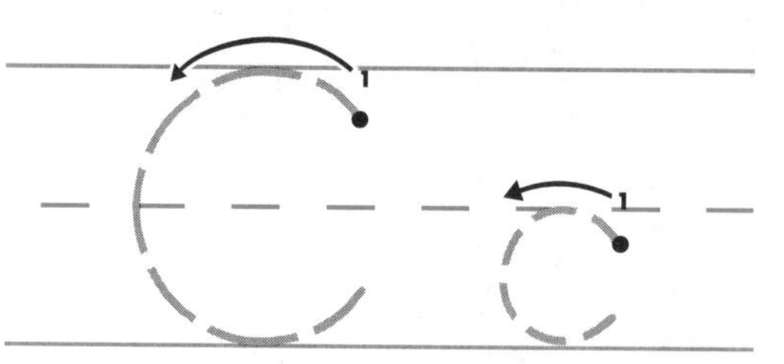

Here are three words that start with **C** or **c**. Can you say them aloud?

Can **come** **came**

Read the story below, and then circle all the words that start with **C** or **c**.

Carmen was so happy. She had a new friend. Her new friend said, "**Can** you **come** over and play?"

When Carmen arrived, her friend said, "I'm so happy you **came** over to play!"

Doggie D!

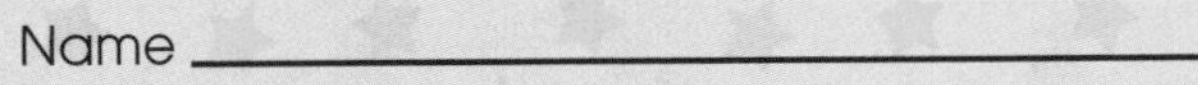
Name ____________________

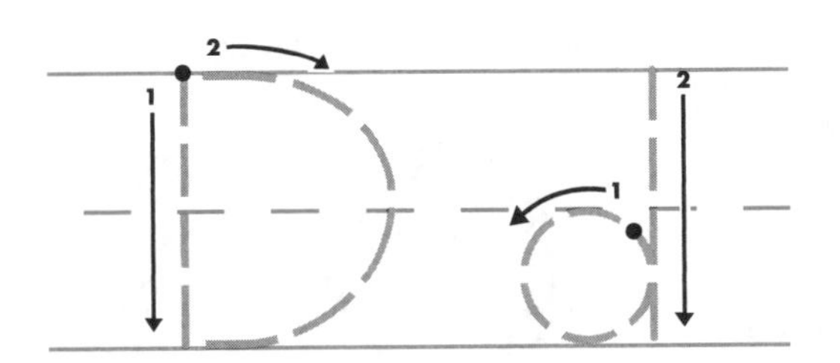

What is the first sound you hear when you say **dog**? What other pictures on the page begin with the same sound?

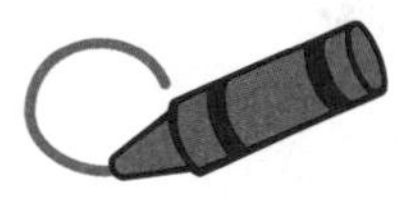
Circle the pictures with a crayon, and then say each one.

Tell a story about the diving dog in the picture.

Here are three words that start with **D** or **d**. Say them aloud. Then trace the **D** or **d** in each word.

Down

Did

do

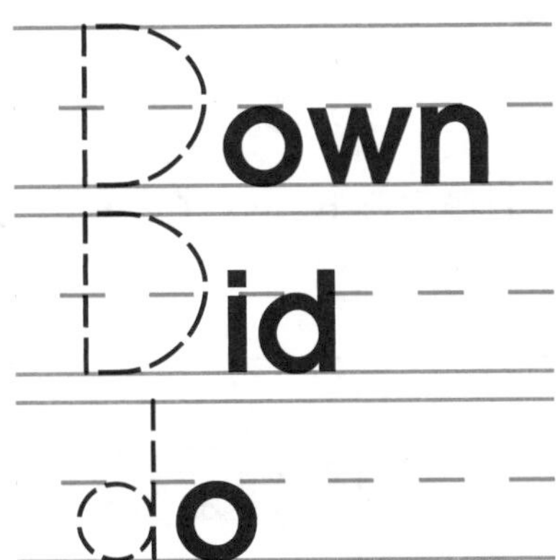

Name ______________________________

Eggbert Eats His Eggs!

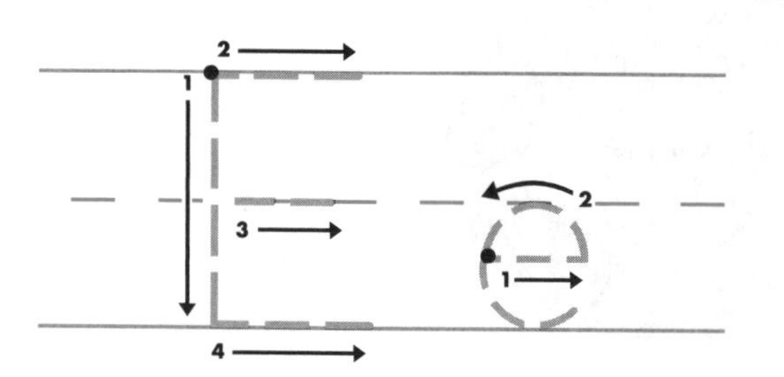

eat
Egg

Before Eggbert will eat his eggs, he likes to color them.

Look at the eggs below and color them.

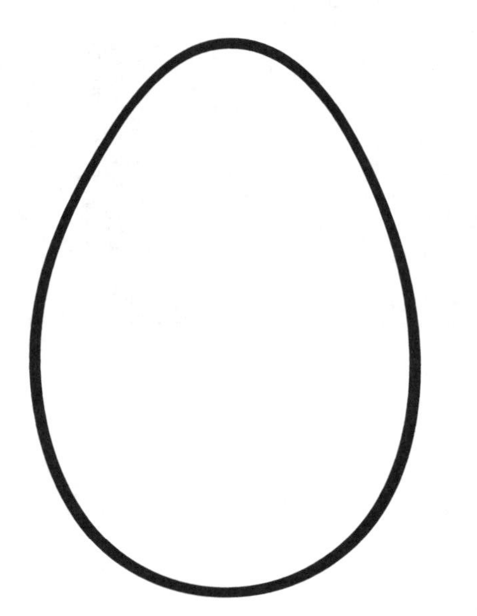

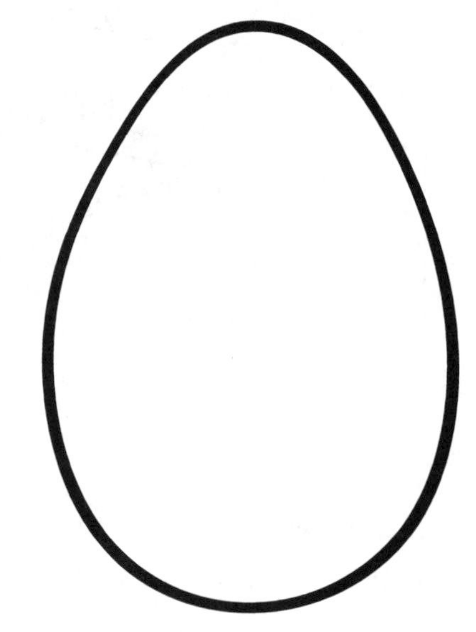

Trace the dotted **E** or **e** in each word below. Then say the whole sentence!

Name ______________________

Funny Fours!

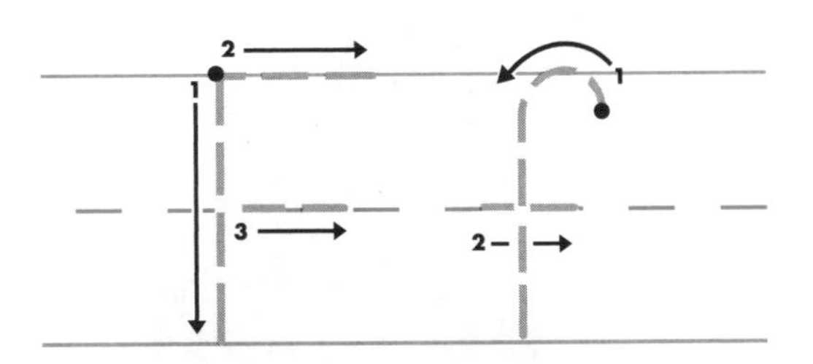

Here are four words that start with **F** or **f**. Say the words aloud, and then trace the dotted **F** or **f** in each word.

Find

four

funny

For

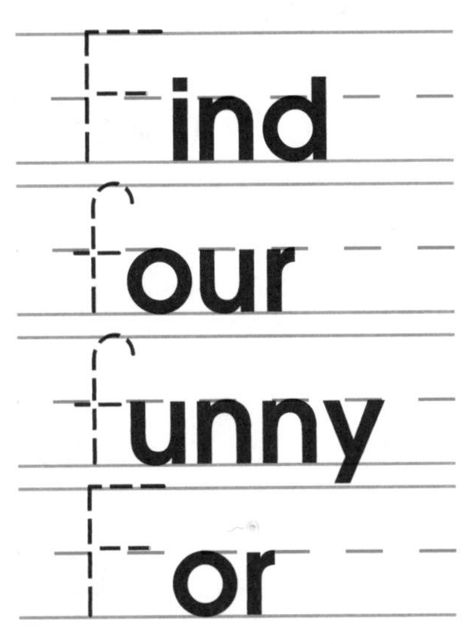

Can you find four funny fours?! Circle them.

Go!

Name ______________________________

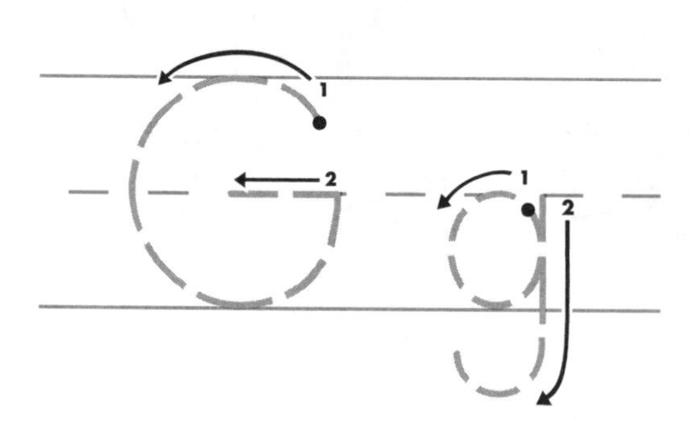

Gabe will **go** to the grocery store.
He will **get** grapes that taste **good**!

Look at the words below, and then say them aloud.

Go Trace the **G** in **Go**:

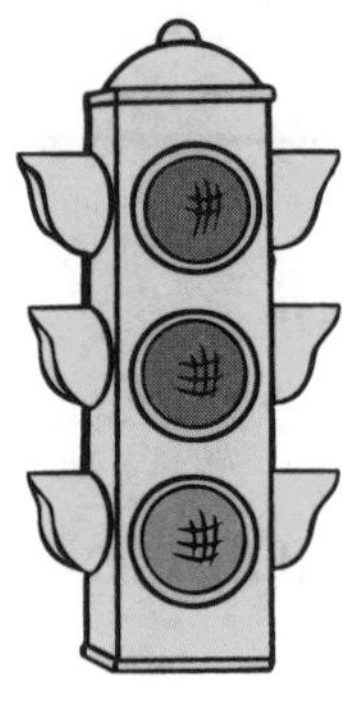

get Trace the **g** in **get**:

Good What is something good to eat?

____

Draw a picture in the box below of something good!

Name ______________________________

Hats Off!

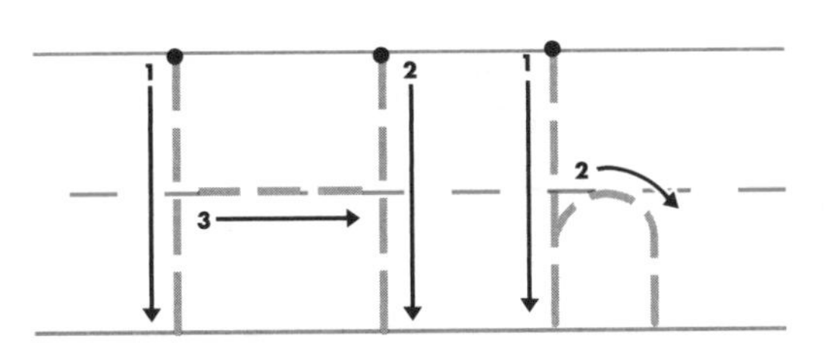

Look at the hat in the box above. What other pictures on the page begin with the same sound? Circle them and say each new word aloud.

Here are some words that start with **H** or **h**. Say the words aloud, and then trace the **H** or **h** in each word.

Help

here

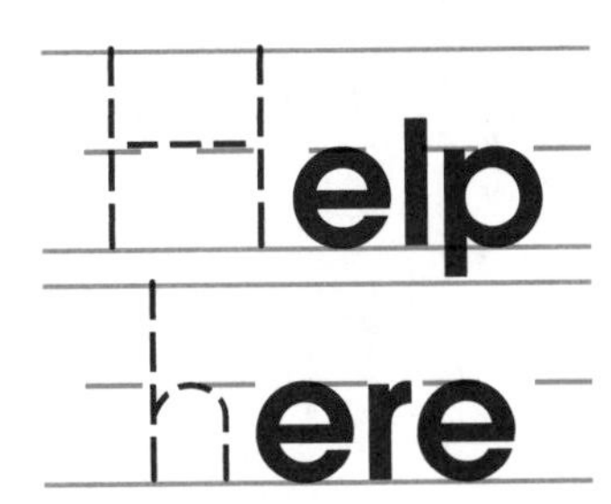

Name ______________________________

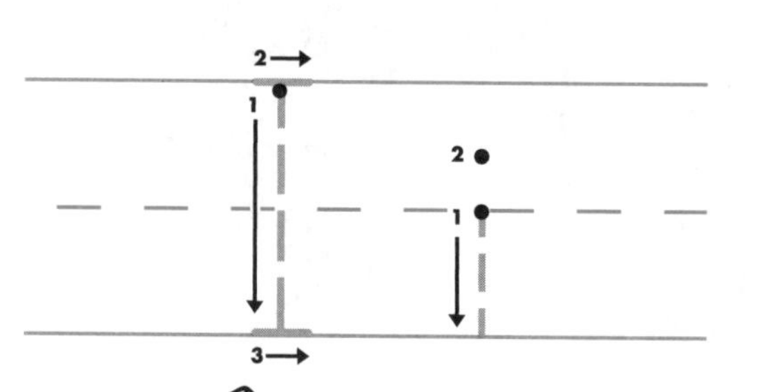

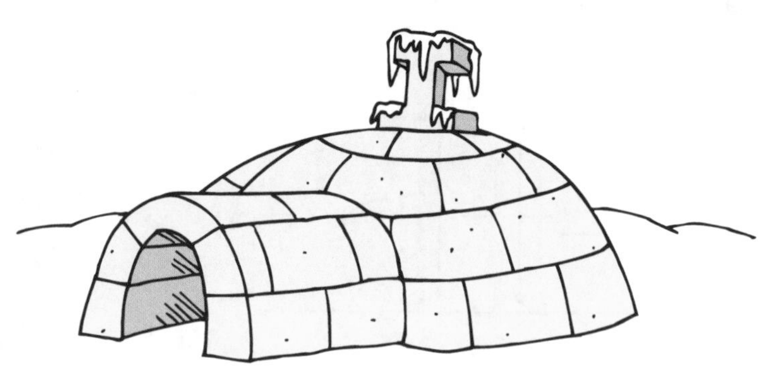

Read the words below, and say them aloud. Then trace the **I** or **i** at the beginning of each word.

I

in

is

It

into

I went **into** an igloo to visit my penguin friends.
It sure was cold **in** there! **I** said, "This **is** for the birds!"

Draw a picture of the igloo.

Name ______________________________

Jumpin' Jars!

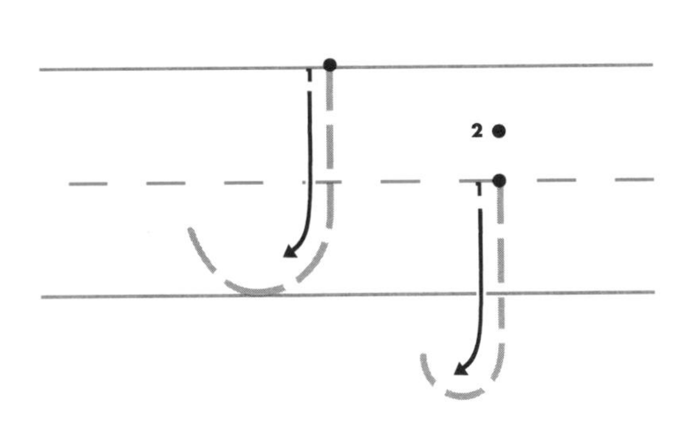

Jump

Something jumped out of the jar! What do you think it was?

Trace the **J** in **Jump** and the **j** in **jar**.

Now draw a picture of what jumped out of the jar!

Can you jump?

Name ____________________

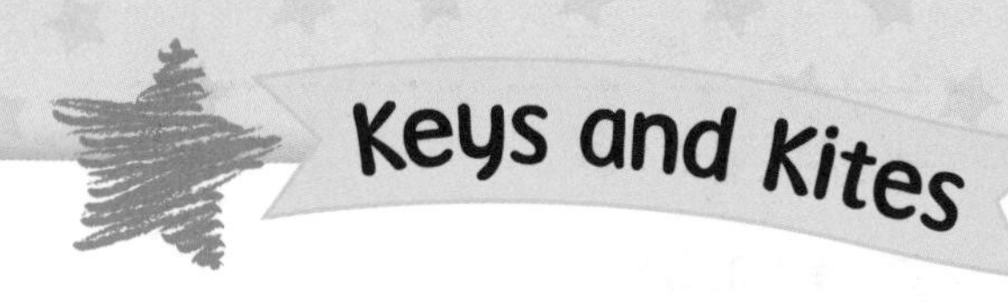

Keys and Kites

Look at the picture in the box below. Say aloud what it is.

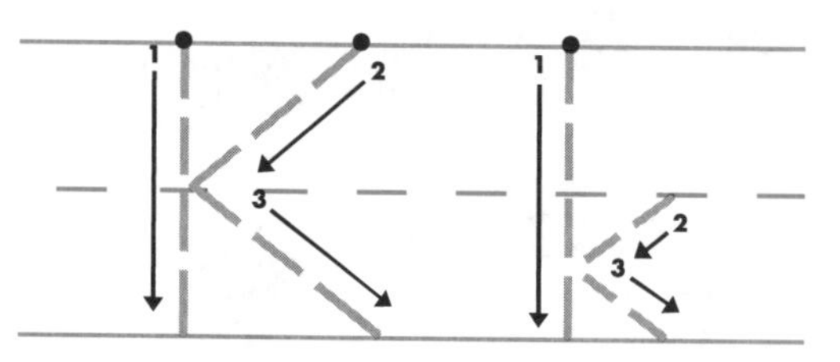

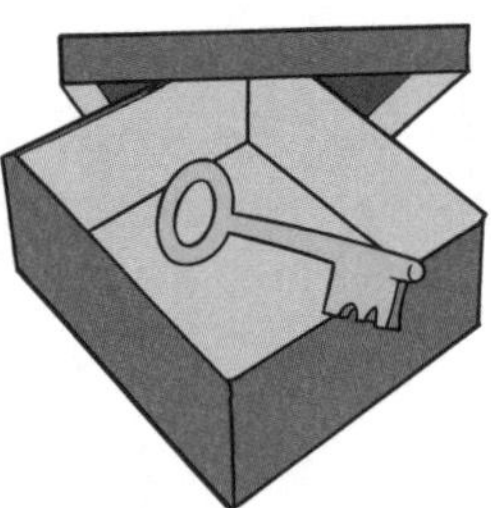

Look at the three pictures below. Circle the picture that has the same sound as the picture in the box.

Can you think of a new word that starts with **K**? Say it aloud, and then draw a picture.

Leaping Lizards!

Name ____________________

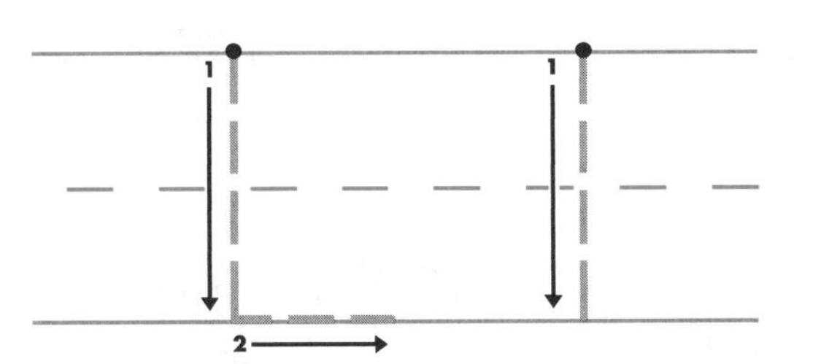

Circle the picture below that starts with the same sound as **lizard**.

"**Look** and see if you **like** that **little** lizard," said my mom. "If you do, we will take him home."

"Leaping Lizards! I love him!" I said. And that's how I got my very own lizard.

Say each word aloud. Then trace the letter **L** or **l** in each word.

Look L ook

like l ike

little l ittle

Name ____________________

Monkey in the Middle!

Look at the picture in the middle of the page. What is it? Name all the pictures on the page.

Then color all the pictures red that start with the same sound as the picture in the middle of the page.

Say each word aloud. Then trace the **M** or **m** in each word below.

make I **make** my bed. make

me Let **me** help you. me

My **My** pet is friendly. My

The Missing N!

Name ____________________

Each person is missing something that begins with the letter **N** or **n**. Read the sentences aloud.

Now draw a nose for the man. Draw a nail for the builder. Draw a neck for the woman. Draw a necklace for the queen.

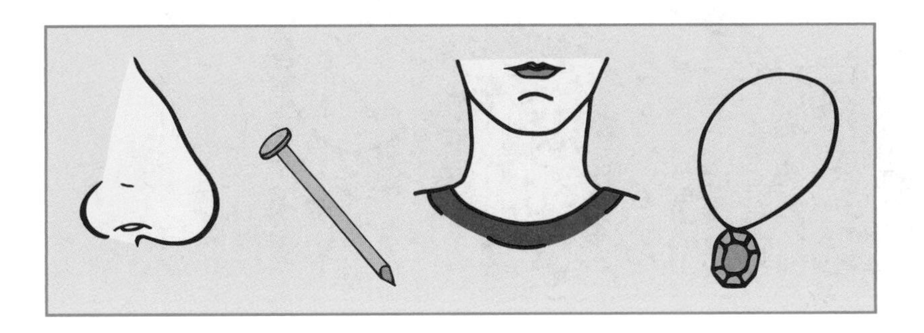

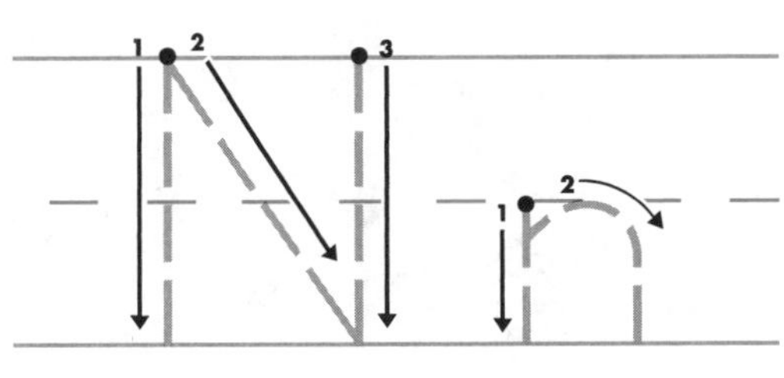

Now I need a nose!

I have **no** neck!

Something is **not** right!

Where is my **new** necklace?

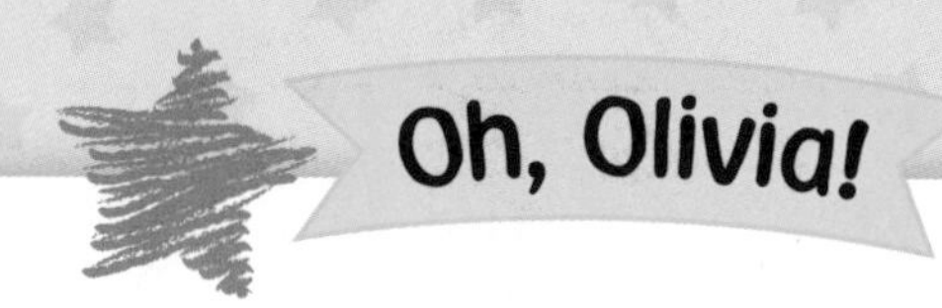

Oh, Olivia!

Name ______________________

One day a little girl named Olivia sat **on** an octopus! The octopus was not happy and said, "You must get **off** me, or I will get **out of** the ocean and sit **on** *your* head!"

"Oh my," said Olivia. And she promised never to sit **on** an octopus again!

One	**on**	**off**	**of**	**out**

Say the words in the word box aloud.

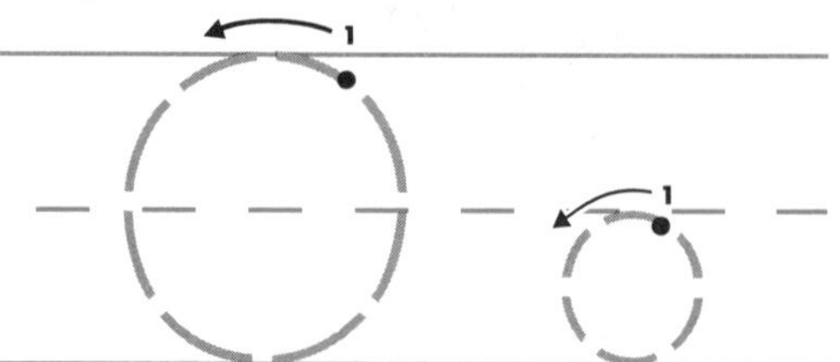

Draw a picture of Olivia, the octopus, and the letter **O** and **o**.

Name ____________________

Peter and the Piano

Peter is a great piano player. He plays **pretty** songs on the piano. People always say, **"Please**, **play** us a song."

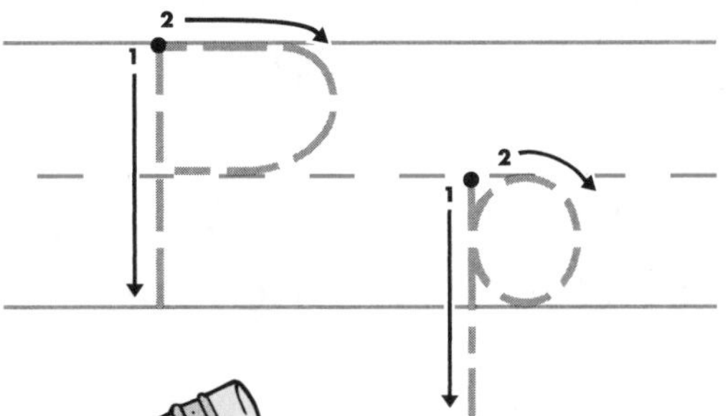

Say these words aloud. Then trace the letter **P** and **p** in each word.

play

pretty

Please

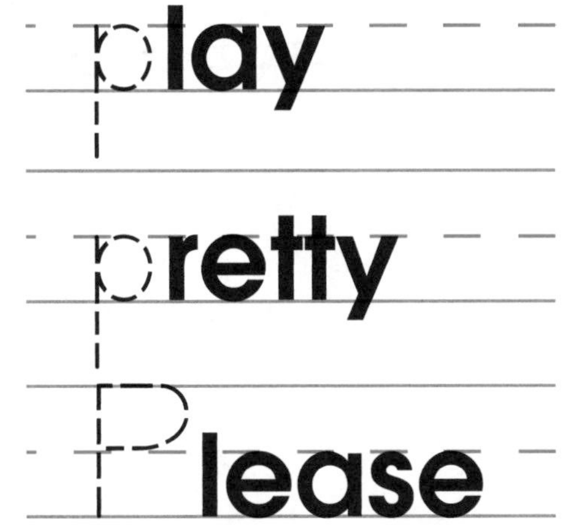

Can you make up a story using these three words? Say your story aloud. Then draw a picture about your story.

Name ______________________________

Queen Quackers!

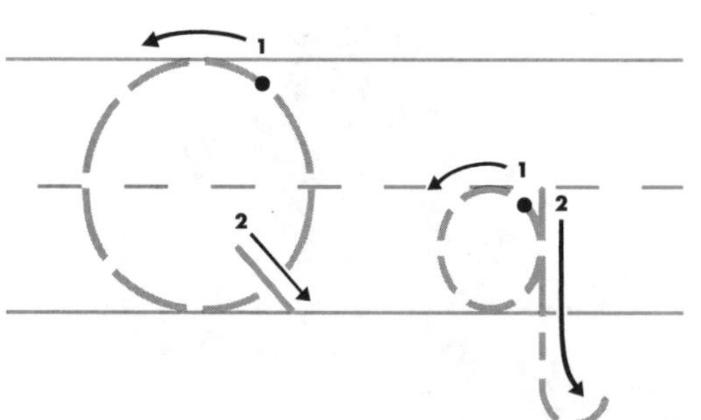

One day the queen's palace was flooded with water. Even though water was rushing into the palace, she refused to leave her throne!

Draw a picture of what happened to the queen.

Name ______________________________

R and **r** are hidden in the picture below. Look carefully to find 4 of them. Then circle them!

Read this sentence aloud.

Ray has a **red** car.

Now trace the **R** in **Ray** and the **r** in **red**.

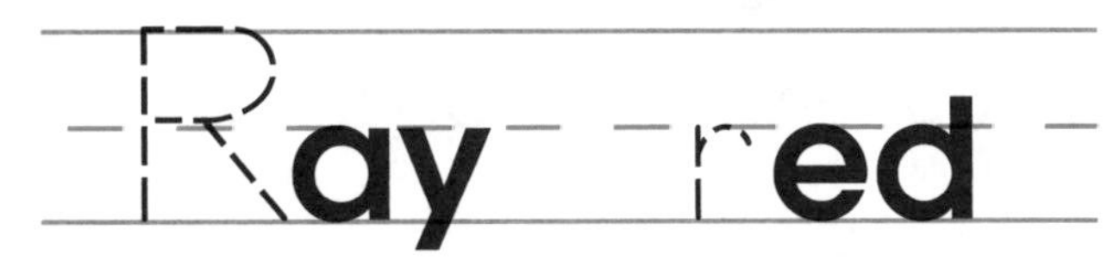

Hidden Pictures

Name ______________________________

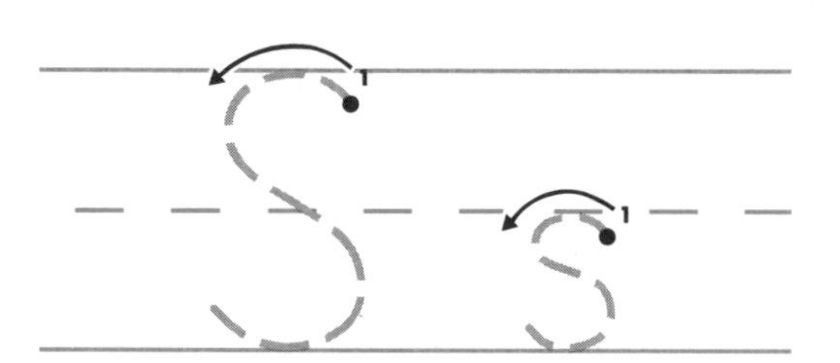

There are lots of things that begin with the letter **S** or **s** that are hidden in the picture below. Can you find a snake, a shark, a shoe, a spider, a star, a snail, and a stamp?

 Circle what you find!

Make up a story about one of the objects that you circled. Why was it hiding?

Hidden Pictures

Name ______________________________

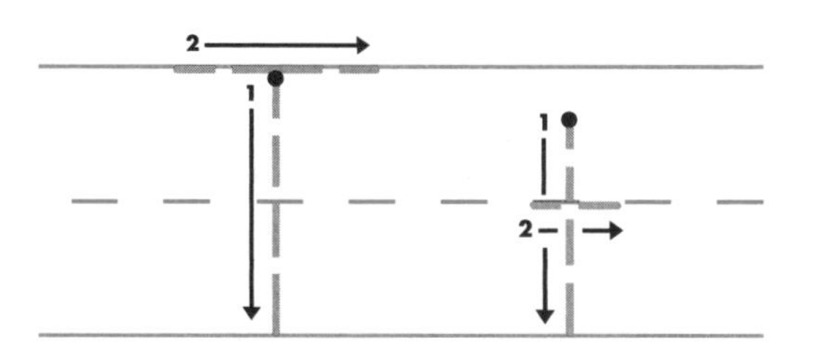

There are lots of things hidden in the picture below that begin with the letter **T** or **t**. Can you find a table, a tooth, a tiger, a top, and a tie?

Circle what you find.

What are the two kids talking about on the Ferris wheel? Make up a story about them!

Name ______________________

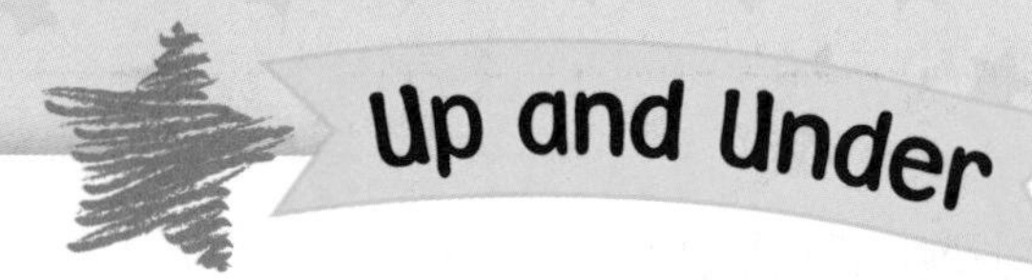

Trace the **U** in the word **Up**.

Now trace the **u** in the word **under**.

Name ________________________________

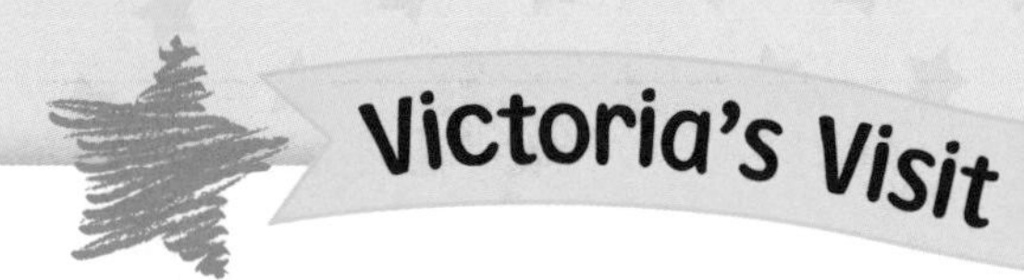

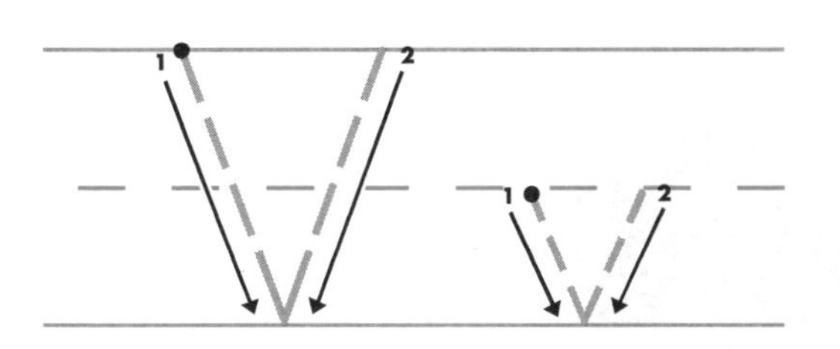

Victoria visited her friend Violet. Violet's house is very messy. Help Victoria and Violet find her violin, her mother's favorite vase, and the vacuum cleaner.

 Circle the pictures, if you can find them!

Do you know of a place that is very messy? Tell a story about it.

Name ____________________

All the pictures on this page begin with the letter **W** or **w**.

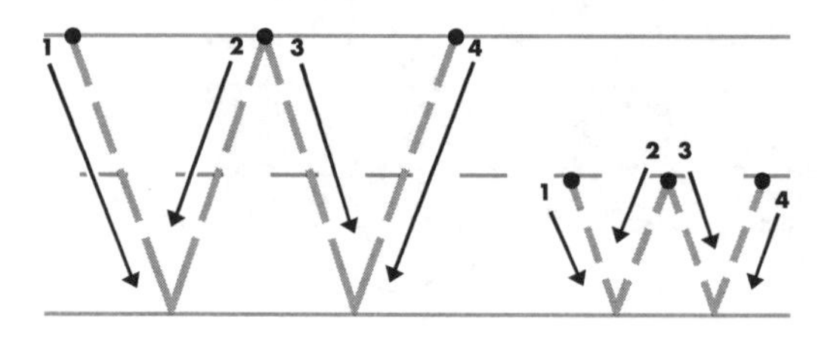

Find something to serve at breakfast. What is it?

Find something that is round. What is it?

Find something that squirrels like to eat. What is it?

Find something that wiggles. What is it?

Find something that lives in the ocean. What is it?

Name ______________________

Read the sentences below. Pay special attention to the **W** and **w** words!

______ **What** does the bear **want** to eat? Is he feeling **well**? Draw a picture of your answer.

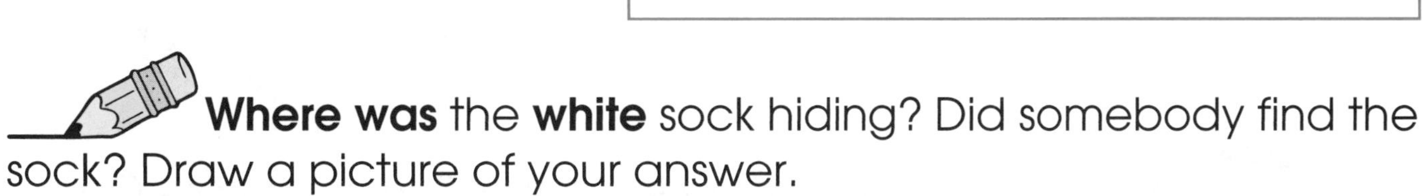

______ **Where was** the **white** sock hiding? Did somebody find the sock? Draw a picture of your answer.

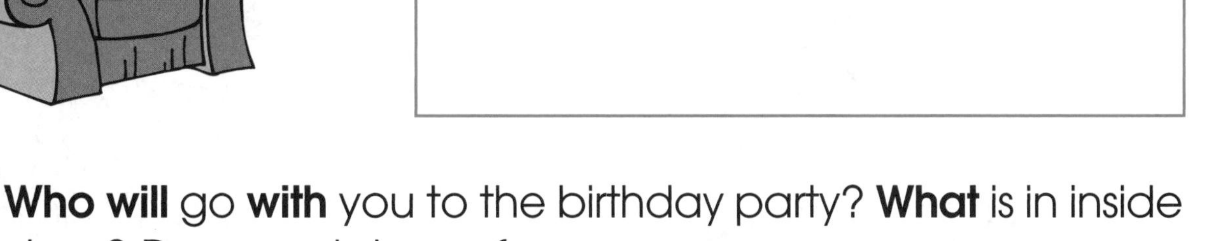

______ **Who will** go **with** you to the birthday party? **What** is in inside the pretty box? Draw a picture of your answer.

Letters and Lines

Name ______________________________

 Color the **X** and **x** green.

 Color the **Y** and **y** yellow.

 Color the **Z** and **z** purple.

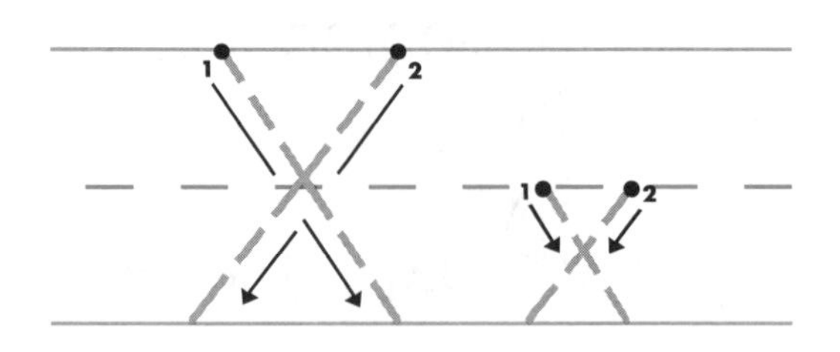

Zz

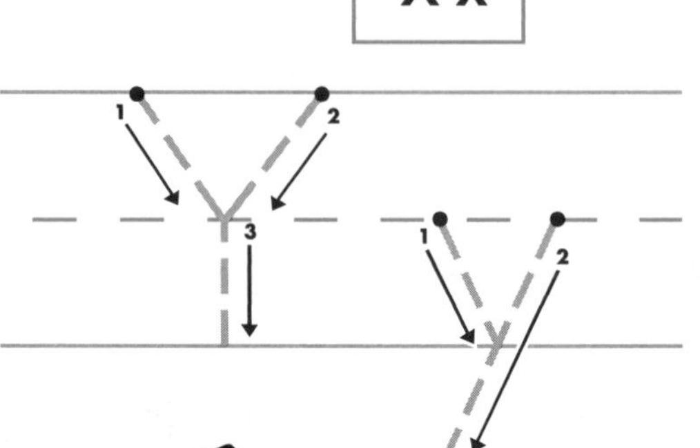

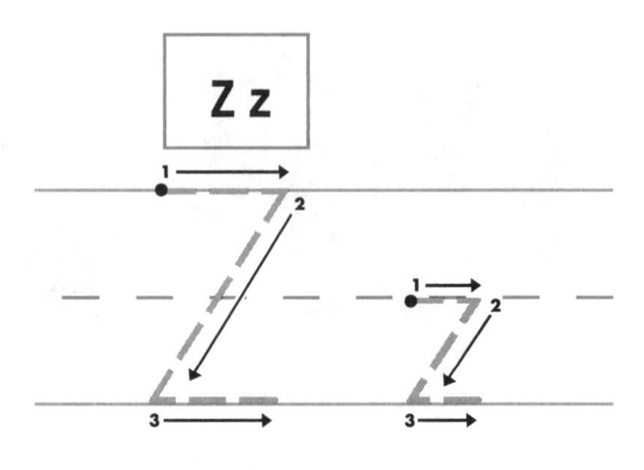

Have you ever seen a **yellow** zebra? **Yes**? Uh, oh! Color the other zebra using its correct colors!

Name ______________________________

Mixed-Up Letters

Draw a line from each letter below to the animal whose name begins with that letter.

O P I

Z V Y

Name ______________________

Missing Letters!

Look at each caterpillar. Write the letter that comes **between** the two letters in the alphabet.

Name ___________________________

Circle Clues

Find the secret word. Read all the clues. Then write each letter in the correct balloon.

C is on top.
N is on the bottom.
L is under C.
O is in the middle.
W is on top of N.

What word did you spell?
Tell a story about the picture. Who do you think the balloons are for?

Name ____________________

Your Very Own Letter!

What letter does your name begin with? Write that letter in the picture frame below. Make it as big as you can. Draw a colorful design in the space around the letter.

Can you think of some words that begin with the same letter as your name?

Name ________________________________

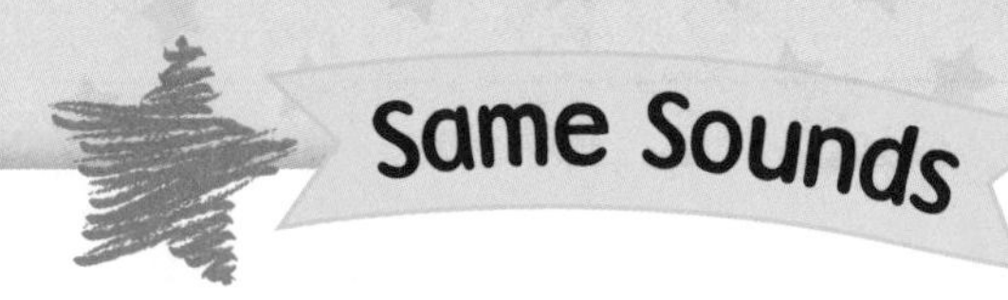

Rhyming words are words that sound the same.

Say the names of the pictures in each row. Circle the pictures that rhyme in each row.

Name ______________________

Puppy Talk

Look at the puppy below. Parts of it are labeled. Say the names of the words aloud.

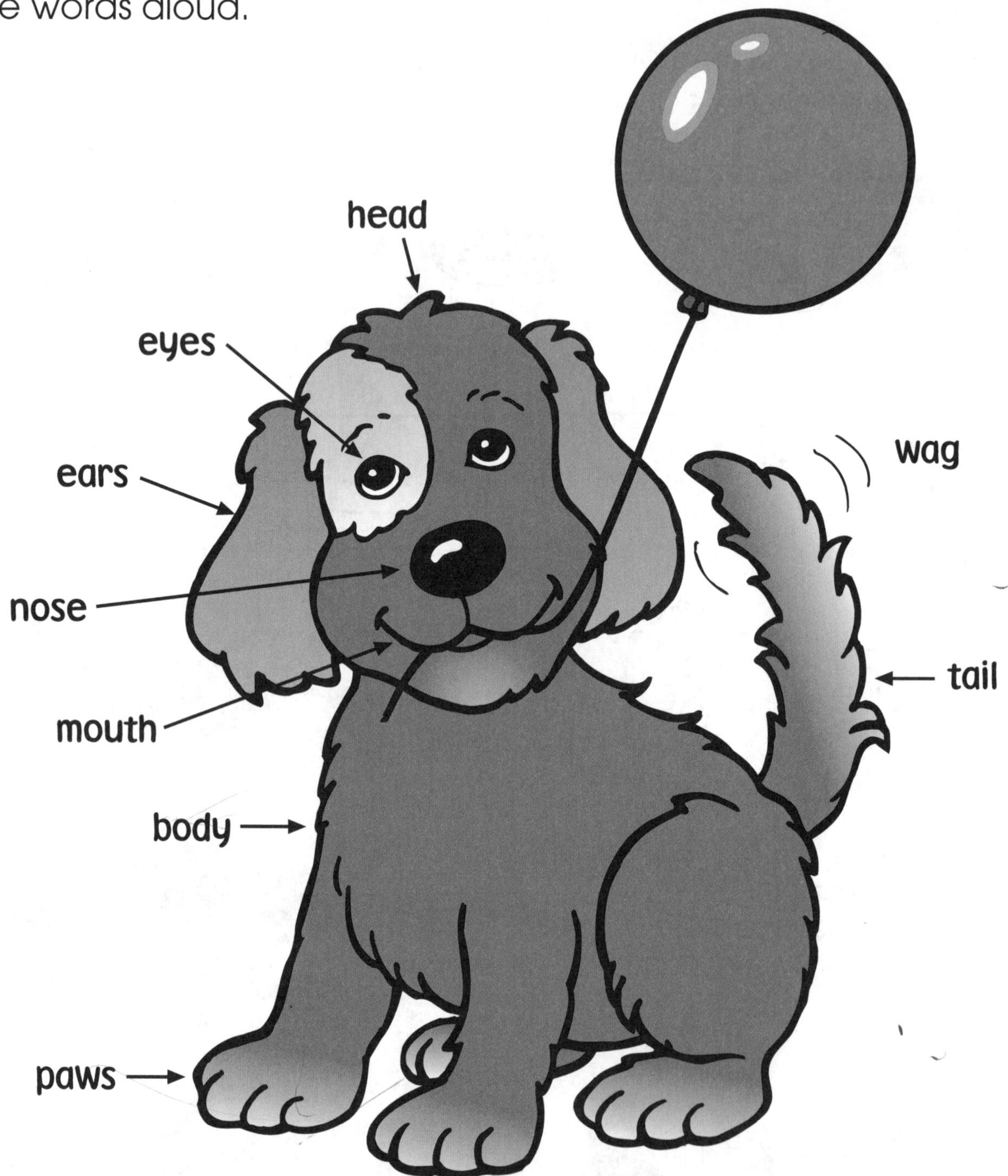

Make up a story about the puppy. Why is it holding the balloon?

Name ______________________________

Look at the picture of the face. Read aloud all the names of the parts found on a face.

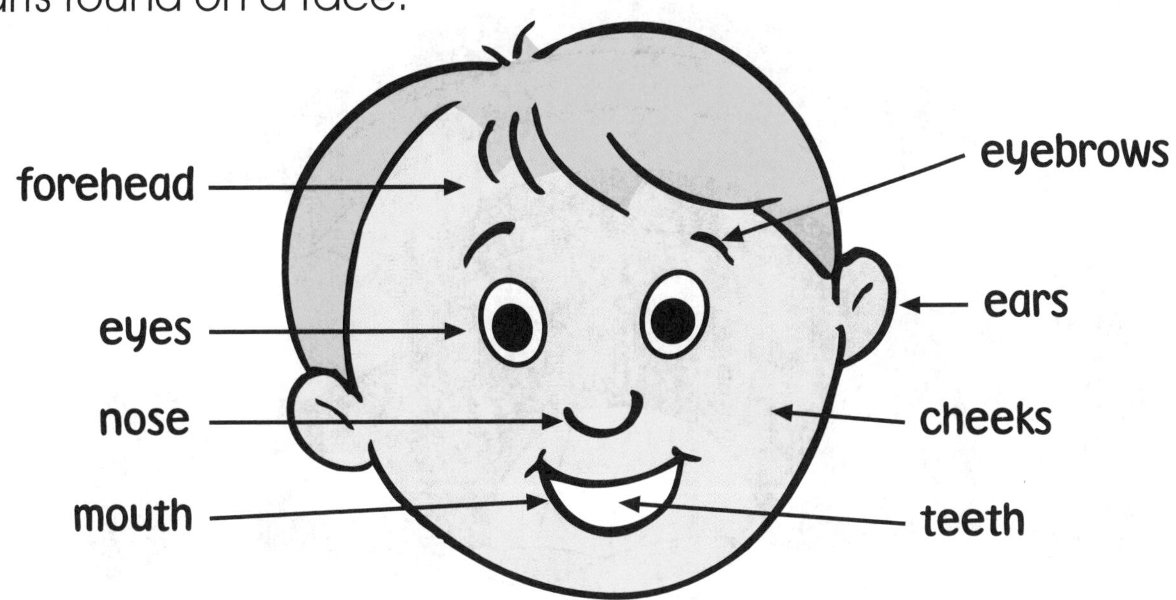

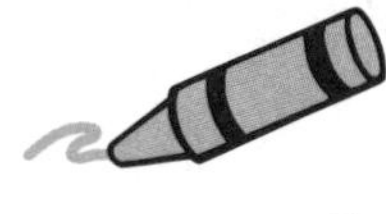 Color this eye and add some eyelashes. 

 Circle the nose that you like. 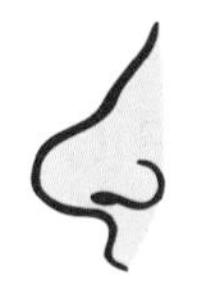  

 Circle the ears that you like. 

 Draw some teeth. 

 Draw a picture of a face.

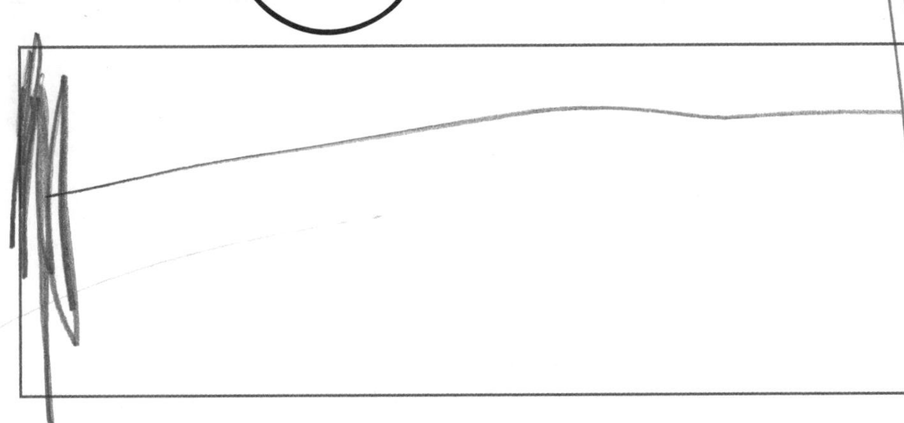

Name ______________________

Look at the rainbow below. Read aloud the names of all the colors in the rainbow.

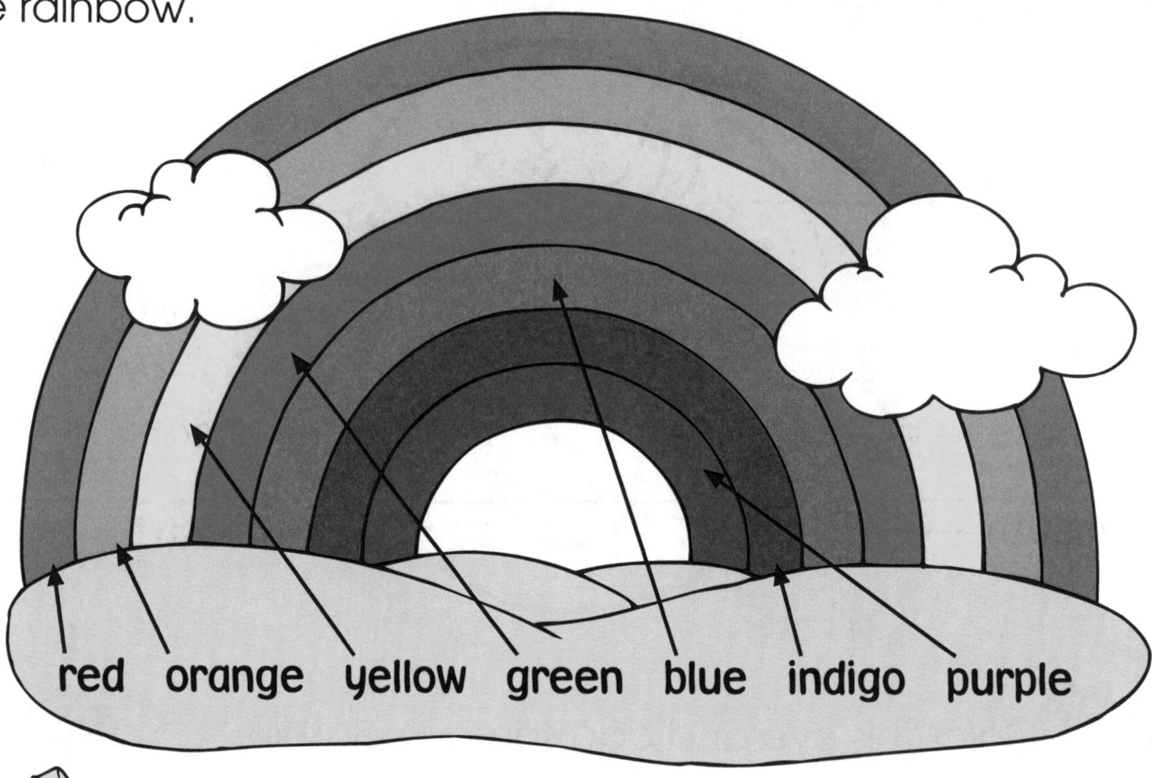

On the line below, write the name of your favorite color.

____

Use a crayon to draw a picture. Color it your favorite color.

Name ______________________

My Best Friend

Draw a picture of your best friend playing with an animal.

Write a sentence about your drawing. Don't forget to use your best friend's name.

____

____

Name ____________________

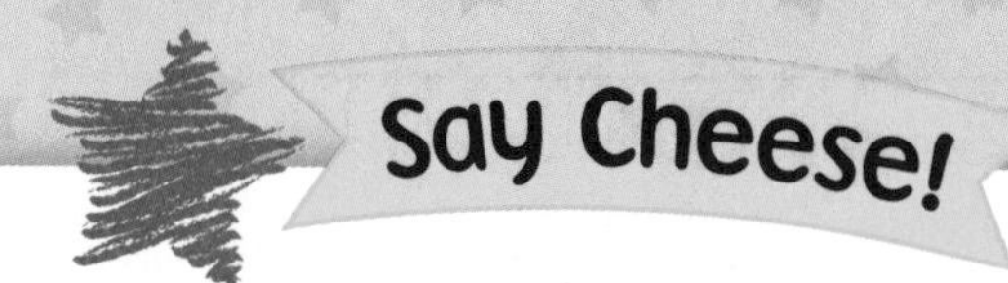

Say Cheese!

What is this picture about? Circle your answer.

a book   a photo   a song

Trace the word below.

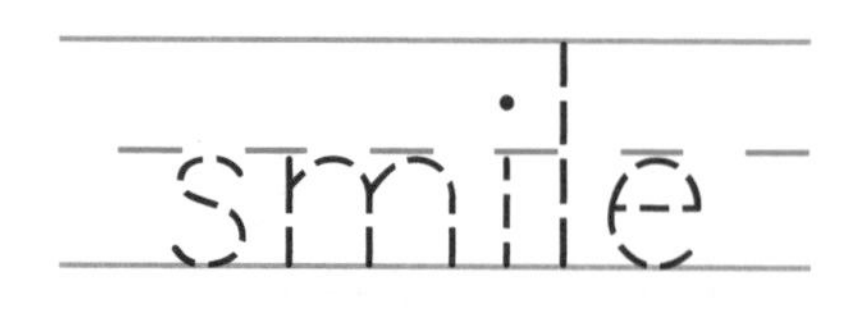

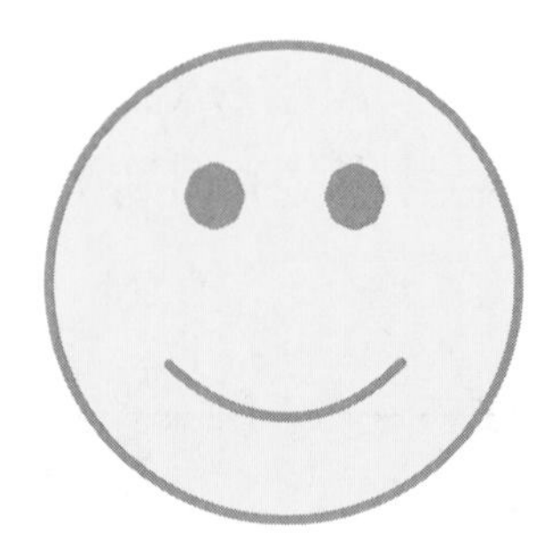

What makes you smile?

Name ______________________________

What's Up?

What food is the cook making? Circle your answer.

apple pie   hot dogs   pizza

Trace the word below. Then say the new word aloud.

What food do you find very yummy?

Name ____________________________

What are the girls putting on their food? Circle the correct answer.

mustard   ketchup   sugar

Trace the word below and say it aloud.

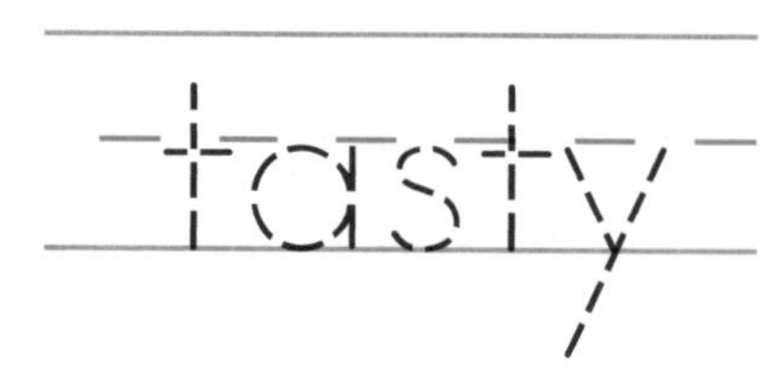

What do you put on your French fries?

Name ______________________

Signs and Symbols

When pictures are used to stand for words, they are called **symbols**. Look at the symbols below. Say each word aloud. Then read the message in the box.

Write the messages on the lines.

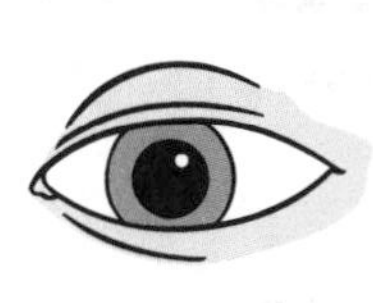  

What does this message say?

 ______________________

 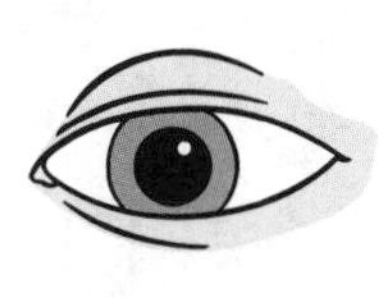  

What does this message say?

 ______________________

Secret Codes

Name ______________________________

One day when you and your friends are playing outside, you come across a spooky cave! You walk inside and see pictures on the walls. One of your friends tells you that before people wrote with words, they used pictures to tell stories.

Look at the pictures below. Say each word aloud. Can you figure out what this message is saying?

= hunters

= dream

= under

= stars

____

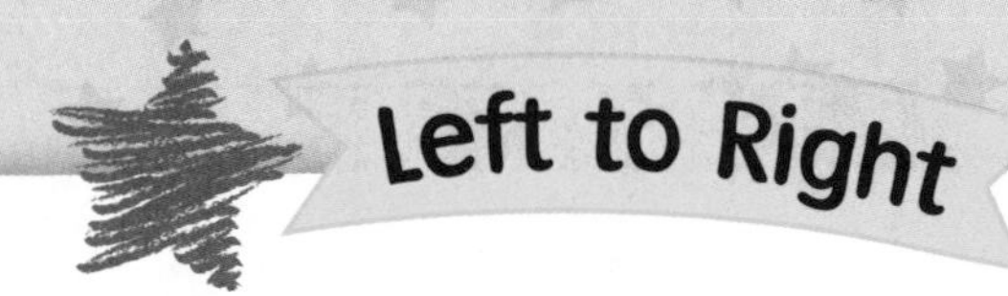

A bee, a man, and an elephant are all learning how to read! Help them learn how to read by tracing your finger over the lines below.

Sentences are read from left to right. Use a crayon to trace the lines from left to right.

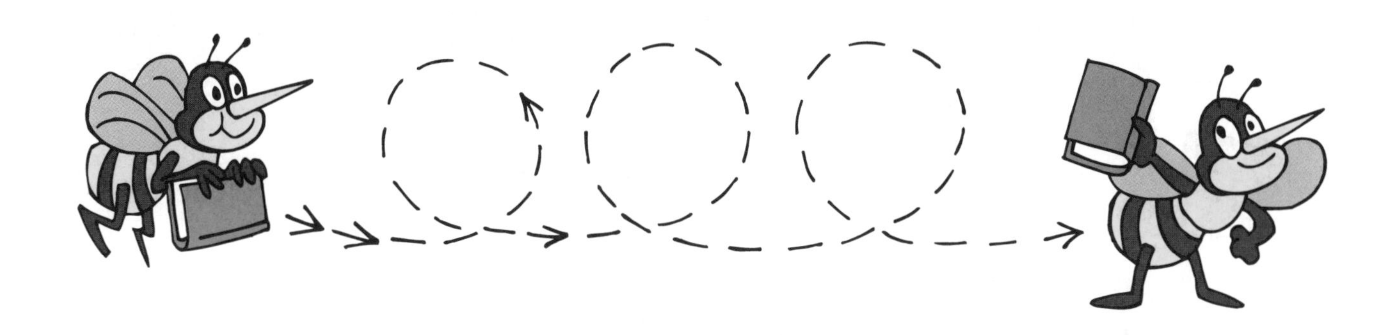

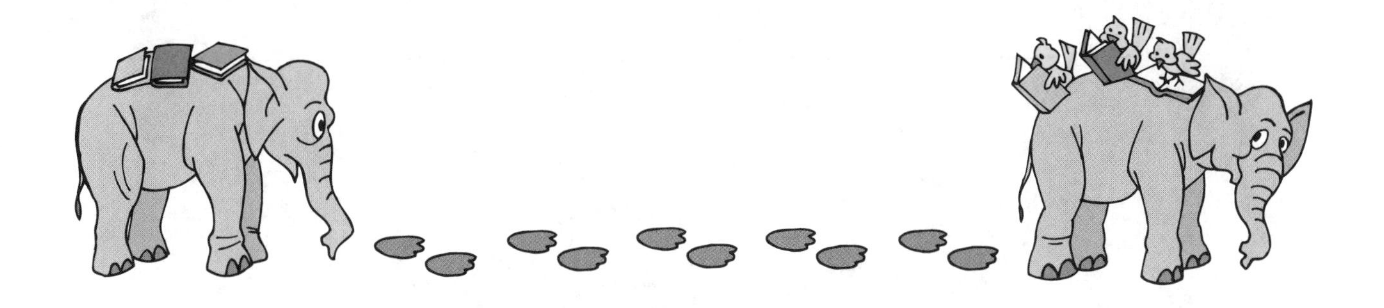

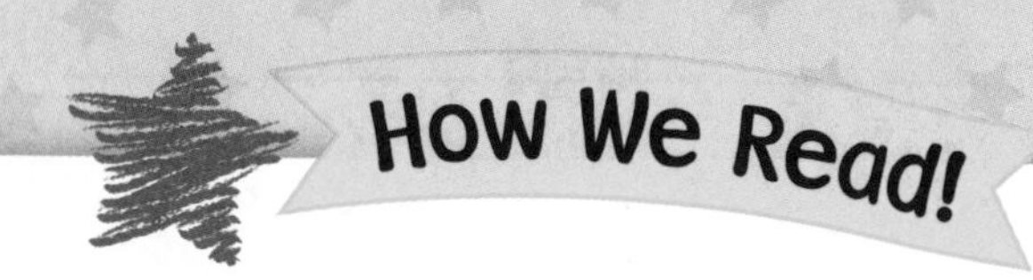

Name ______________________________

Sentences are read one row at a time. Start at the top row. Read the whole sentence from left to right. Then read the next row under it from left to right. Do the same with each next row until you reach the end of the page.

Tell the two bears that they need to eat their ice cream in the same way that we read! They should start at the top and eat one layer at a time.

Use a crayon to draw a path that shows the bears how to eat their ice cream.

Name ______________________

Look at the flower below. Does it remind you of spring? Inside each flower petal are two sets of words. Two words should make you think of spring. The other two words should not.

Circle the two words in each petal that remind you of spring.

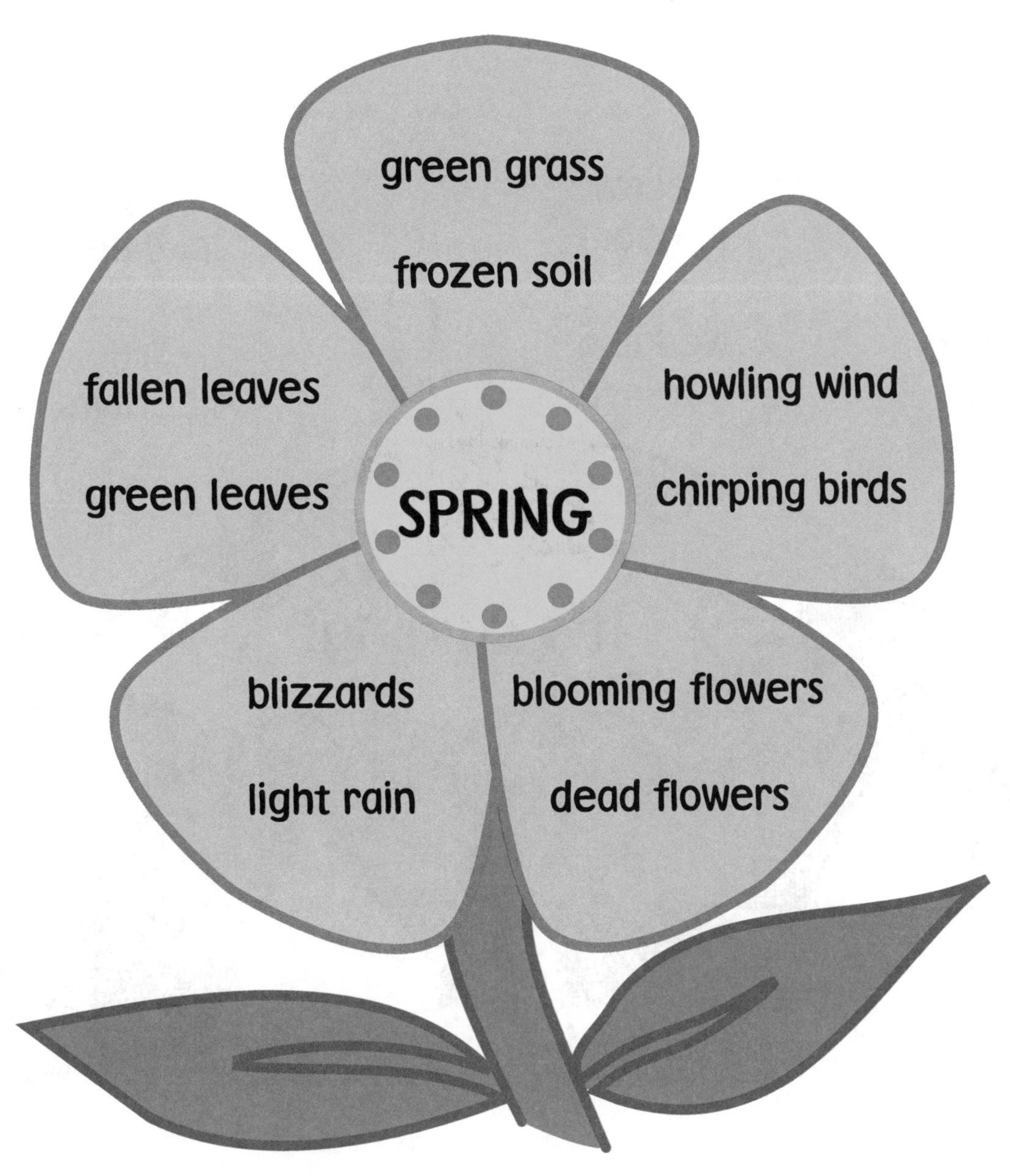

Can you make up a story about what happens in spring?

Raining Again!

Name ______________________________

Around the umbrella are six raindrops. Inside each raindrop are two sets of words. Two words should make you think of rain. The other two words should not.

Circle the words in each drop that remind you of rain. One raindrop is empty for you to fill in.

What do you think about when it is raining?

Name ___________________________

Draw a line to match each pair of rhyming words to its picture. The first one is done for you.

Think of two words that will rhyme and go together to make a silly picture. Example: This is a MUG - BUG !

Here are some words to help you. Try to think of more on your own.

run	**bug**	**fun**	**ball**
tall	**fall**	**rock**	**hug**
top	**sun**	**rug**	**clock**
mug	**sock**	**mop**	**bun**

Now you write two words and draw a picture.

This is a ____________ - ____________!

Name ______________________

Rhyming River

You are on vacation at a house by a river. Look around the house to find the four things that rhyme with **rock**. Circle them.

More Rhyming

Name ________________________________

Draw a line to match each pair of rhyming words to its picture. The first one is done for you.

plum drum ————————————

big fig

rain Jane

rock clock

Name ____________________________

Read this nursery rhyme aloud:

Hey diddle diddle, the cat and the fiddle,
The cow jumped over the moon;
The little dog laughed
To see such fun,
And the dish ran away with the spoon.

What if the cow was too heavy to jump over the moon? What would happen then? Draw a picture of this in the box.

Name ____________________

Miss Muffet

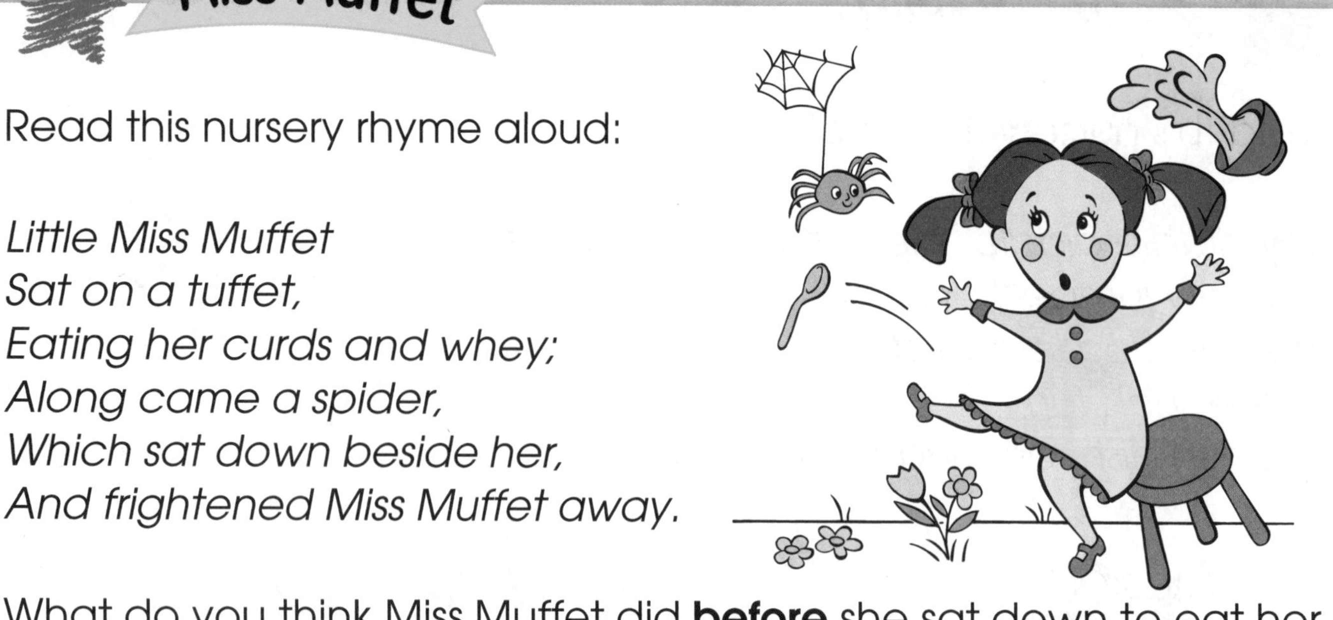

Read this nursery rhyme aloud:

Little Miss Muffet
Sat on a tuffet,
Eating her curds and whey;
Along came a spider,
Which sat down beside her,
And frightened Miss Muffet away.

What do you think Miss Muffet did **before** she sat down to eat her curds and whey?

Draw a picture in the box.

What do you think Miss Muffet will do **after** she runs away?

Draw a picture in the box.

Name ______________________________

Humpty Dumpty

Read this nursery rhyme aloud:

Humpty Dumpty sat on a wall.
Humpty Dumpty had a great fall.
All the King's horses and all the King's men
Couldn't put Humpty together again.

Trace the letters below.

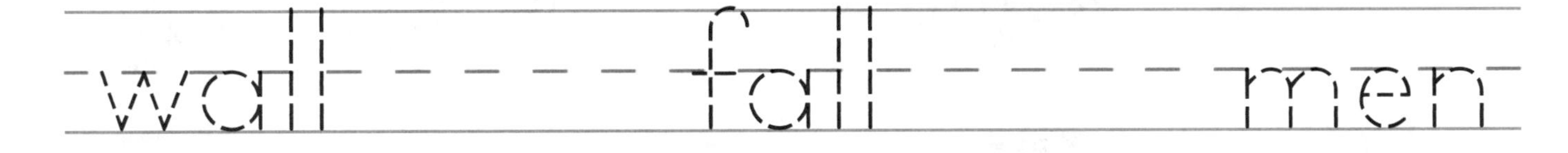

Can you write a sentence with the words **wall**, **fall**, and **men** in it?

____

____

Make up a story with the words **wall**, **fall**, and **men** in it.

Draw a picture of your story.

Name ___________________________

Shopping List

Sam and his mom are at the grocery store. Circle what Sam and his mom should buy.

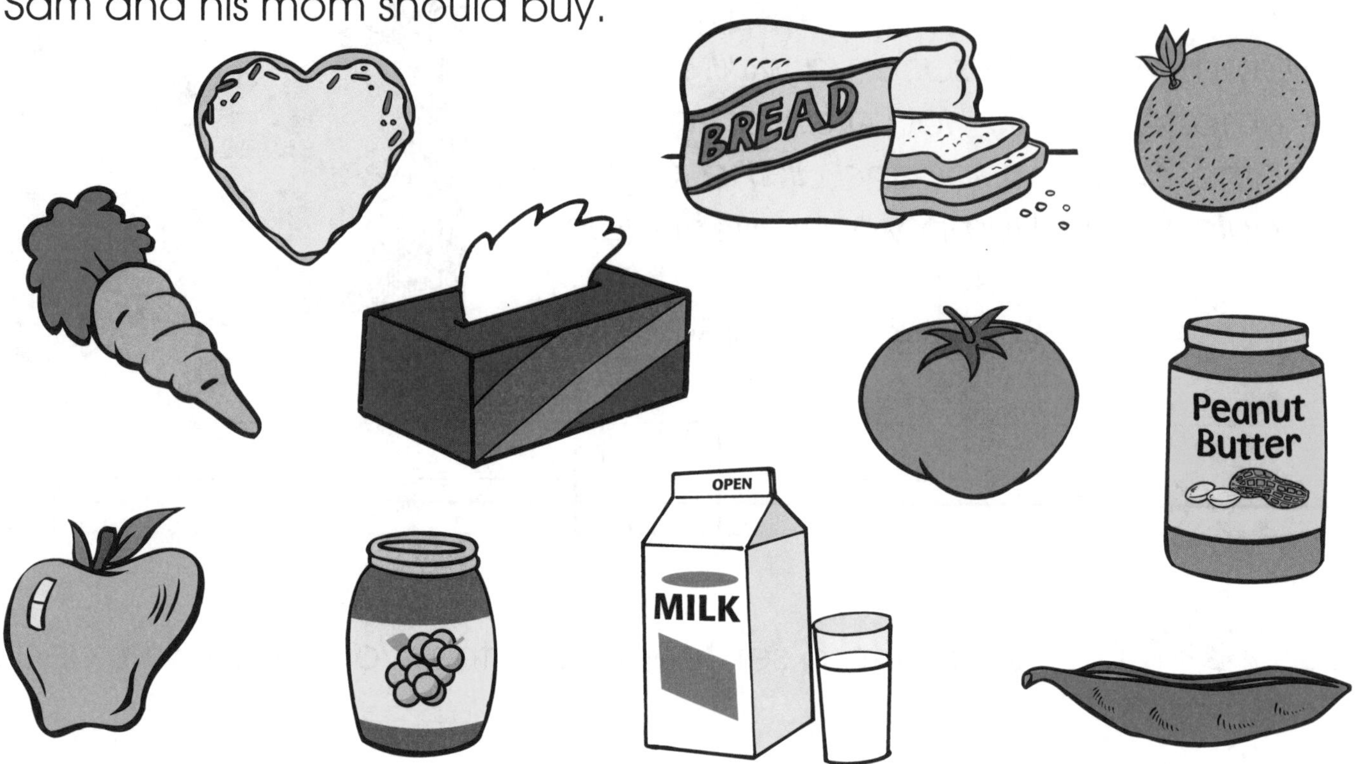

Then say aloud what you would choose to eat for lunch.

On the table below, draw what you would like to eat.

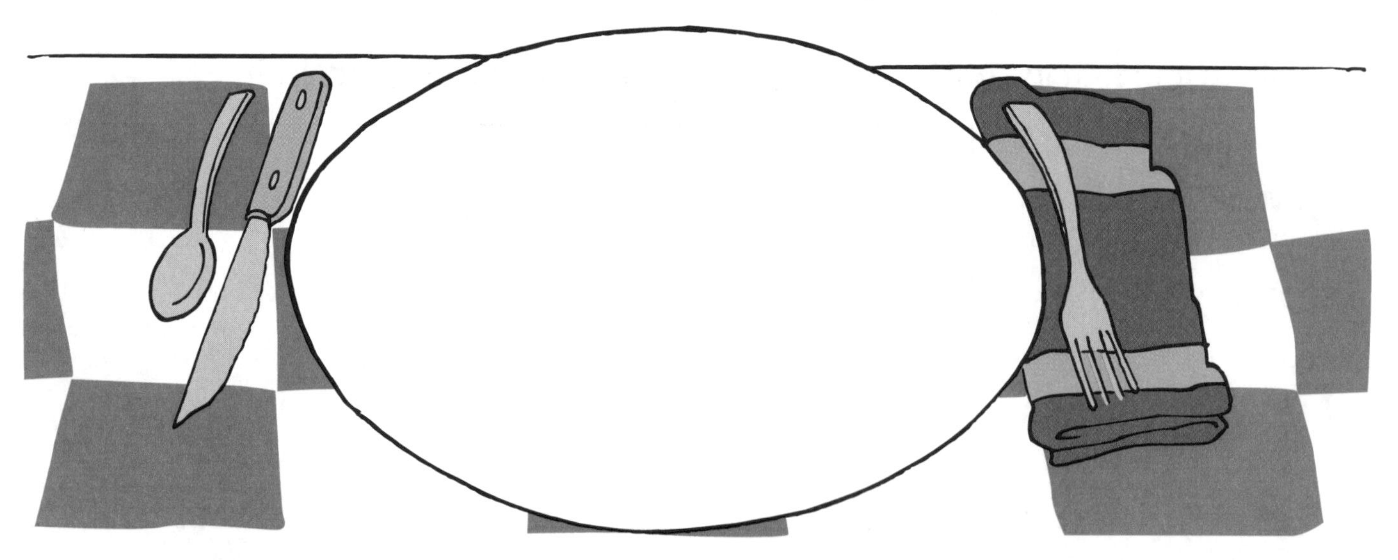

Name ____________________

Homemade Play Dough

Ingredients: 2 cups of flour
1 cup of salt
$\frac{1}{2}$ tablespoon of oil
Water

Directions: As easy as 1, 2, 3!

1. Combine 2 cups of flour and 1 cup of salt.
2. Add 1 cup of water and $\frac{1}{2}$ tablespoon of oil.
3. Mix and knead well. (If too stiff, add more water. If too sticky, add more flour.)

For colored play dough, add vegetable food coloring to the water before combining it with the other ingredients.

Keep in an air-tight container.

Items made from this play dough will become hard in a few days. Then they can be painted.

Name ____________________

Your Turn!

Write a recipe for something new: a party, a handmade gift, a great vacation, or anything you can think of!

My recipe for: ____________________

Ingredients: ____________________

____

____

____

Rainbow Mix

Directions: ____________________

____

____

____

Draw a picture of what it looks like when it's all done.

Newspaper News!

Name ____________________

Chicken Plays the Piano!

Mr. McDonald's chicken is one amazing chicken! Late Thursday night, it was discovered that one of Farmer McDonald's chickens could play the piano!

The chicken sneaked into Farmer McDonald's living room and began pecking on the keys. Soon the chicken was playing a piano concerto!

Farmer McDonald said, "I couldn't believe such fancy music was comin' from the living room and from my very own chicken! That chicken will soon be playing at Carnegie Hall!"

Answer the questions below.
Who was playing the piano?
What happened?
Where did this happen?
When did this happen?
What do you think will happen to the chicken?

Make up a story and draw a picture on a separate sheet of paper.

Bagel Mania!

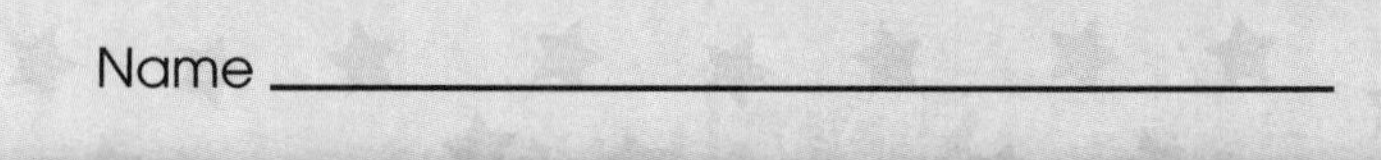

Name ______________________

One day, a bagel fell down from the sky. A note was attached to it. The note said, "I am not a bagel!"

Make a list of all the things it could be besides a bagel. Two are done for you. Have fun!

List

A dinosaur's lost earring

A life preserver for a troll

Name ____________________

One-to-One Connections

Which animals belong together?

Draw a line to connect each mother with her baby.

Each child should be wearing a hat that is the same color as his or her shirt. Which hat should each child be wearing?

Draw a line to connect each child with the correct hat.

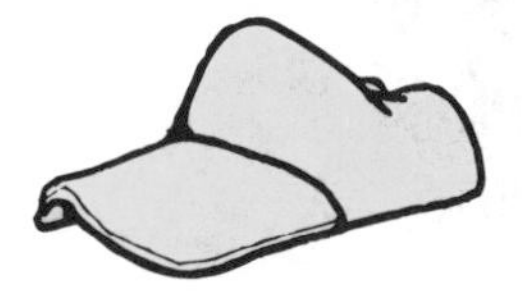

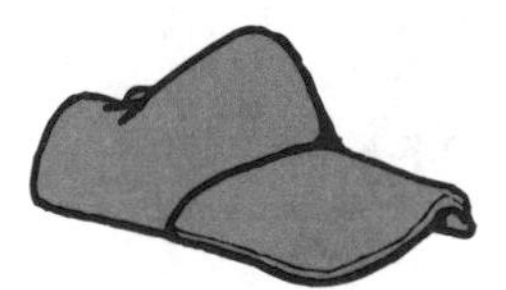

Name ________________________________

More One-to-One Connections

What is missing?

Draw a line to connect each child with the piece of clothing that is missing.

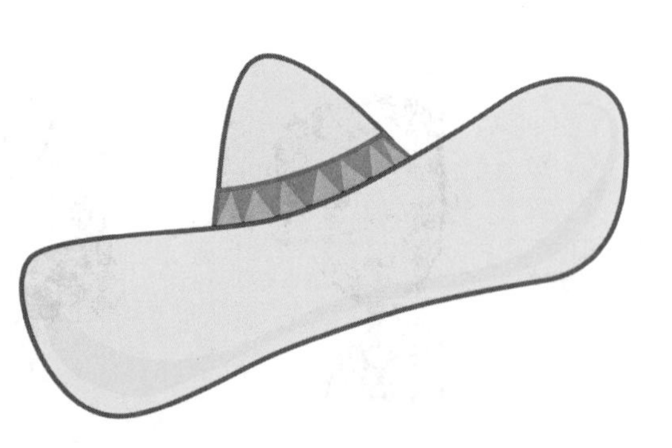

Name ____________________

You Can Count on It!

A corner looks like this:

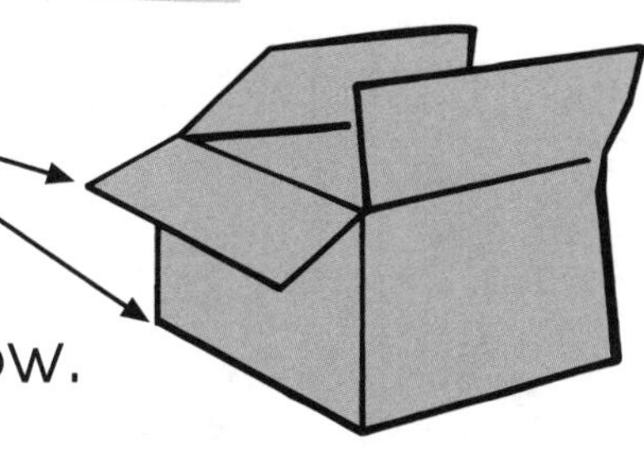

Count the number of corners on each shape below.

Write your answer inside each shape.

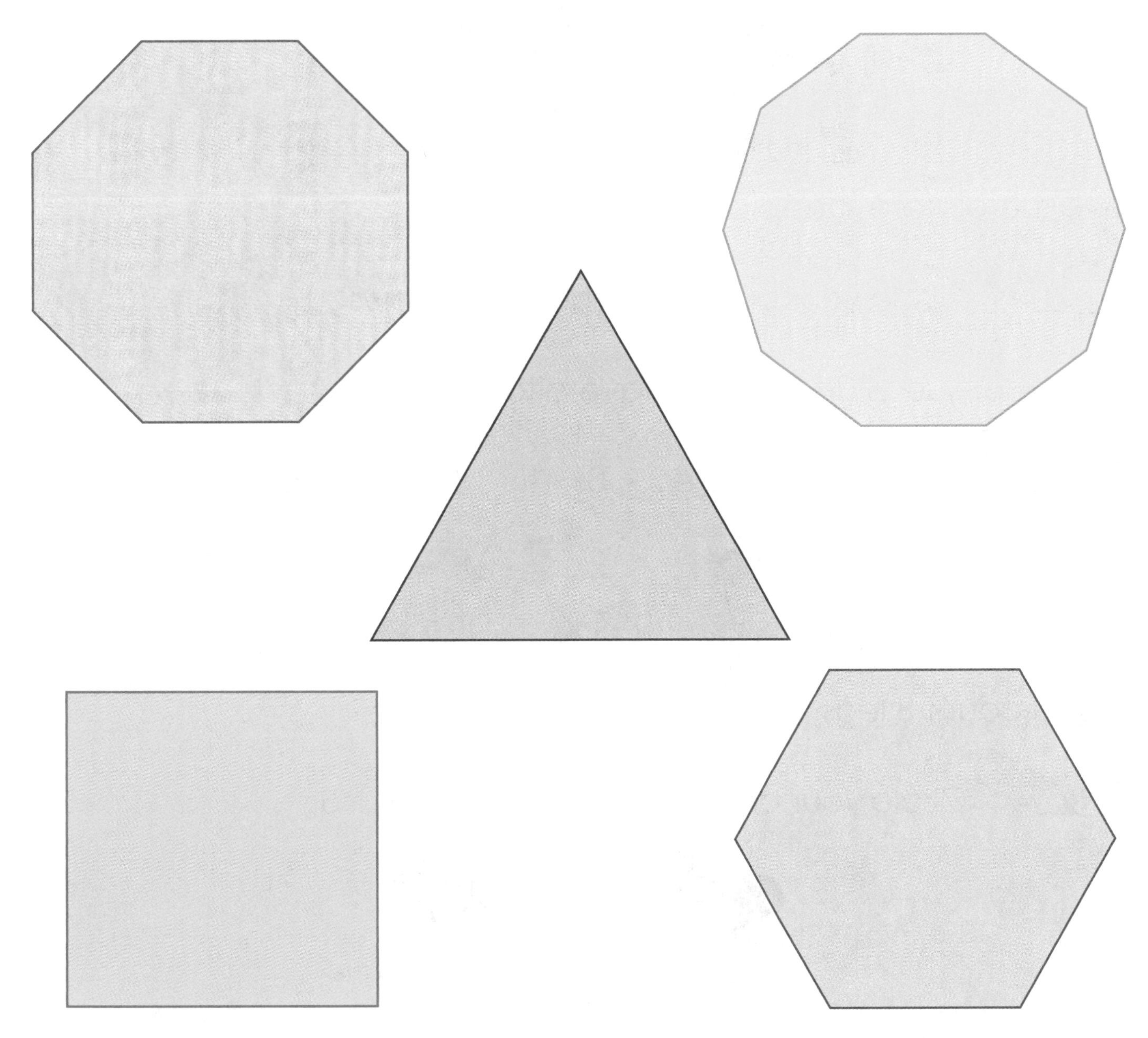

Name ______________________

You Can Count on Me!

How many sheep are in the picture? __________

How many cows are in the picture? __________

Are there more sheep or more cows?

 Circle your answer. sheep cows

How many legs do 3 sheep have altogether?

 Circle your answer. 0 4 8 12 16

If you count 8 legs, how many cows are there?

 Circle your answer. 1 2 3 4 5

Name ____________________

How Many Are There?

How many rows of cars are in the picture?

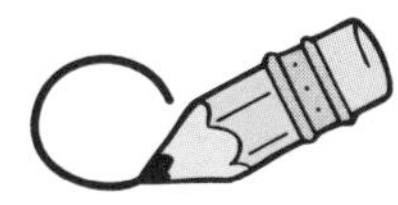 Circle your answer.

1 2 3 4 5

How many cookies are in the picture?

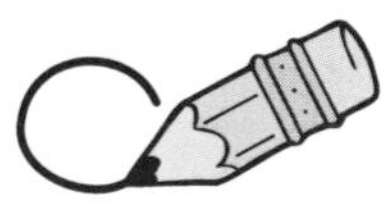 Circle your answer. 1 2 3 4 5

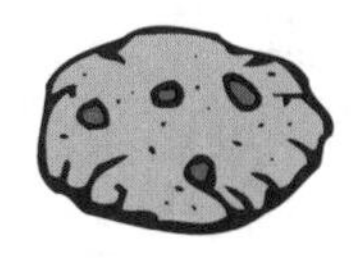

Name ______________________________

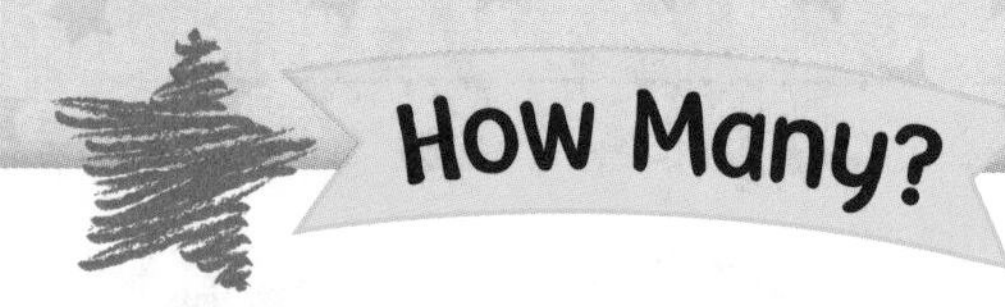

How Many?

How many coins are in the picture?

 Circle your answer.  1 2 3 4 5

How many groups of 5 can be made out of 2 groups of 10?

 Circle your answer. 1 2 3 4 5

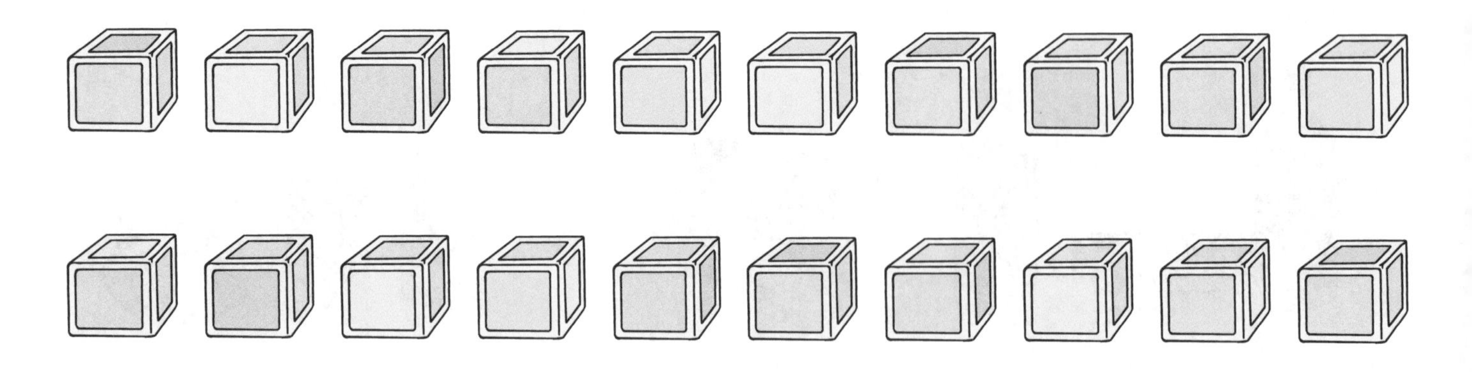

Name ______________________________

Nothing to It!

William has a free pass to see a movie. A movie costs 5 dollars. How many dollars does he have to pay if he uses his pass?

 Circle your answer.

0 1 2 3 4 5

Marie went to a toy store with 20 dollars to spend. She did not spend any money. How many dollars did she take home?

 Circle your answer. 0 5 10 15 20

If you have two nickels, how many more nickels do you need to have a total of 10 cents?

 Circle your answer. 0 1 2 3 4 5

Name ____________________

Billy's mom gave him 5 dollars to play video games at the arcade. At the end of the day, Billy had no money left. How many dollars did he spend at the arcade?

 Circle your answer. 0 1 2 3 4 5

Three plus what number equals 3?

 Circle your answer. 0 1 2 3 4 5

$$3 + ??? = 3$$

Name ______________________________

Parts and Wholes

Which one would you rather have: I piece of a candy bar cut into 3 pieces or I piece of the same-sized candy bar cut into 9 pieces?

 Circle your answer. I piece of 3 I piece of 9

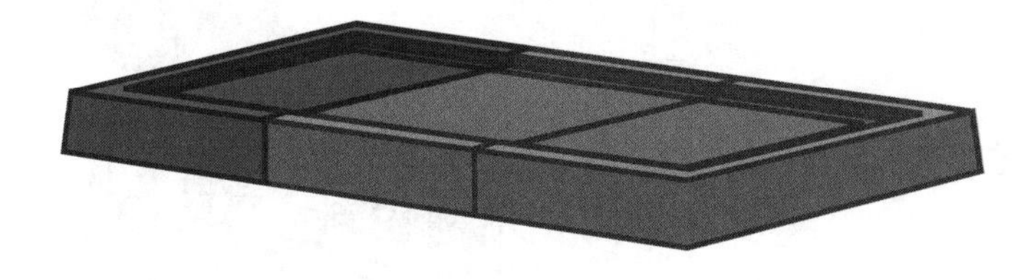

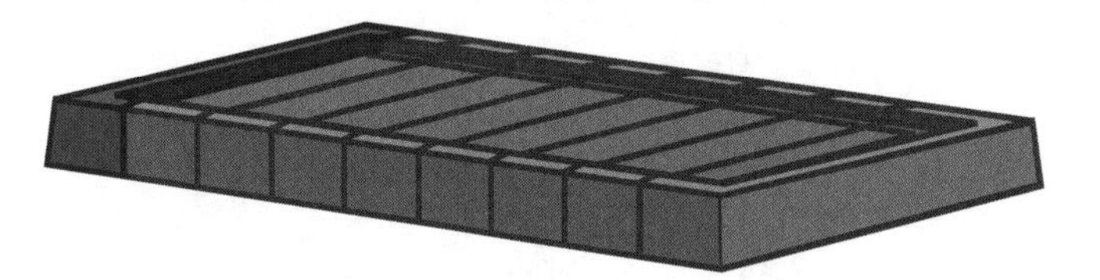

Color half of each shape below. Use a different color for each one.

Name ____________________

More Parts and Wholes

Mom cut a pie into 8 pieces. Her children ate half ($\frac{1}{2}$) of the pie for dessert. How many pieces were left?

 Circle your answer.

Color only half of the circles in each row below. Use a different color for each one.

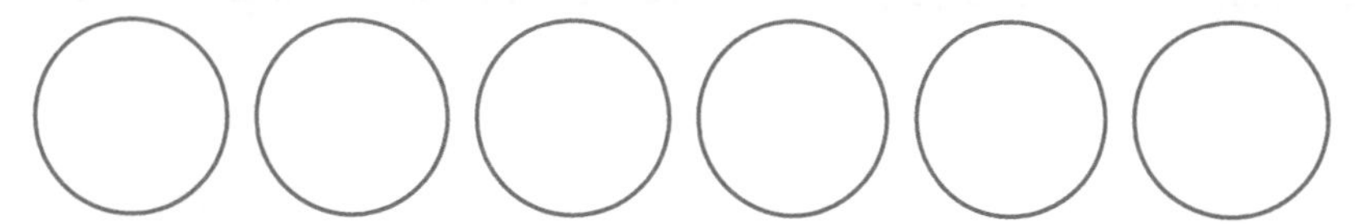

How many circles are **not** colored?

 Circle your answer. 0 1 2 3 4 5 6

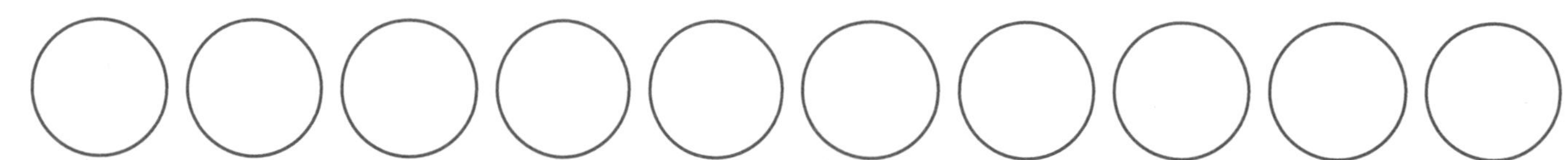

How many circles are **not** colored?

 Circle your answer. 0 1 2 3 4 5 6

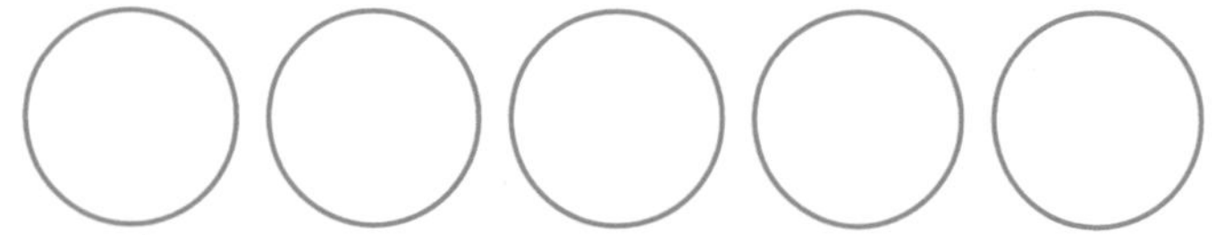

How many circles are **not** colored?

 Circle your answer. 1 $1\frac{1}{2}$ 2 $2\frac{1}{2}$ 3 $3\frac{1}{2}$ 4

Name ____________________

Everybody Into the Pool!

All of the children took off their shoes before getting into the pool. They lined up their shoes in a straight line. How many shoes were there altogether?

  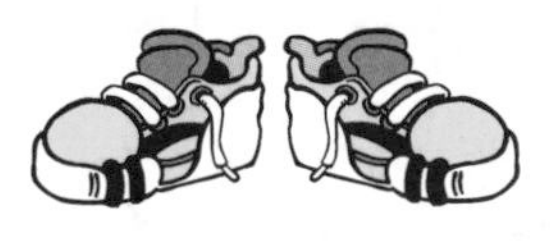  

 Circle your answer. 6 7 8 9 10

How many children are in the pool?

 Circle your answer. 1 2 3 4 5

Some of the children went home. They took their shoes when they left. How many children went home?

 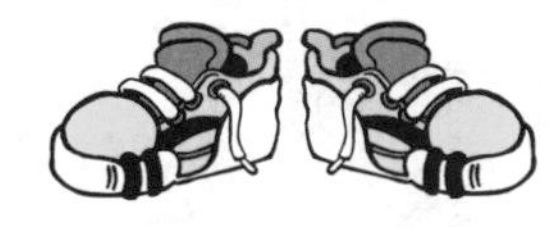 

 Circle your answer. 2 3 4 5 6

On and Off!

Name ______________________________

A bus had 5 passengers.
At the first stop, 5 people got on and 2 people got off.
At the next stop, 4 people got on and 3 people got off.
How many people are on the bus now?

 Circle your answer. 6 7 8 9 10

Another bus started with 4 passengers.
At the first stop, 6 people got on and 4 people got off.
At the next stop, 3 people got on and 2 people got off.
How many people are on the bus now?

 Circle your answer. 6 7 8 9 10

Name ______________________

Clap Your Hands!

Clap your hands three times, pat the top of your head two times, clap your hands three times, and then pause. Repeat this pattern three times.

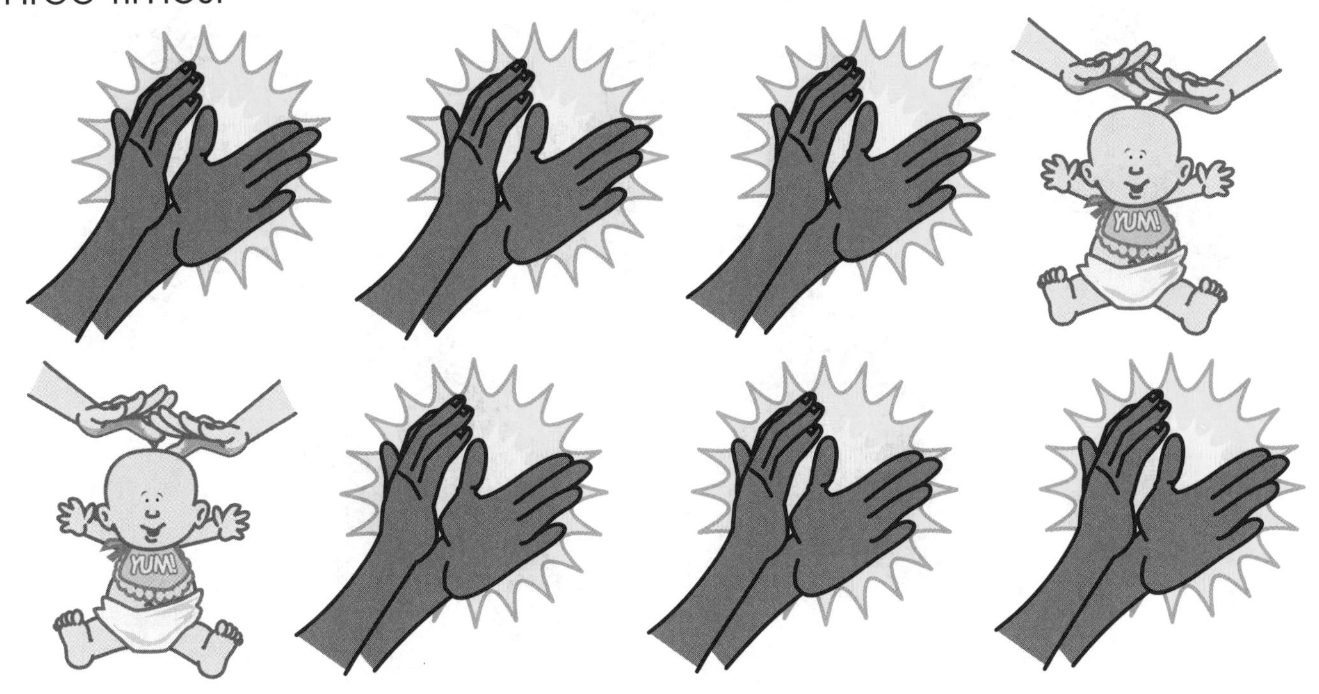

Clap your hands and pat your head as shown in the picture below.

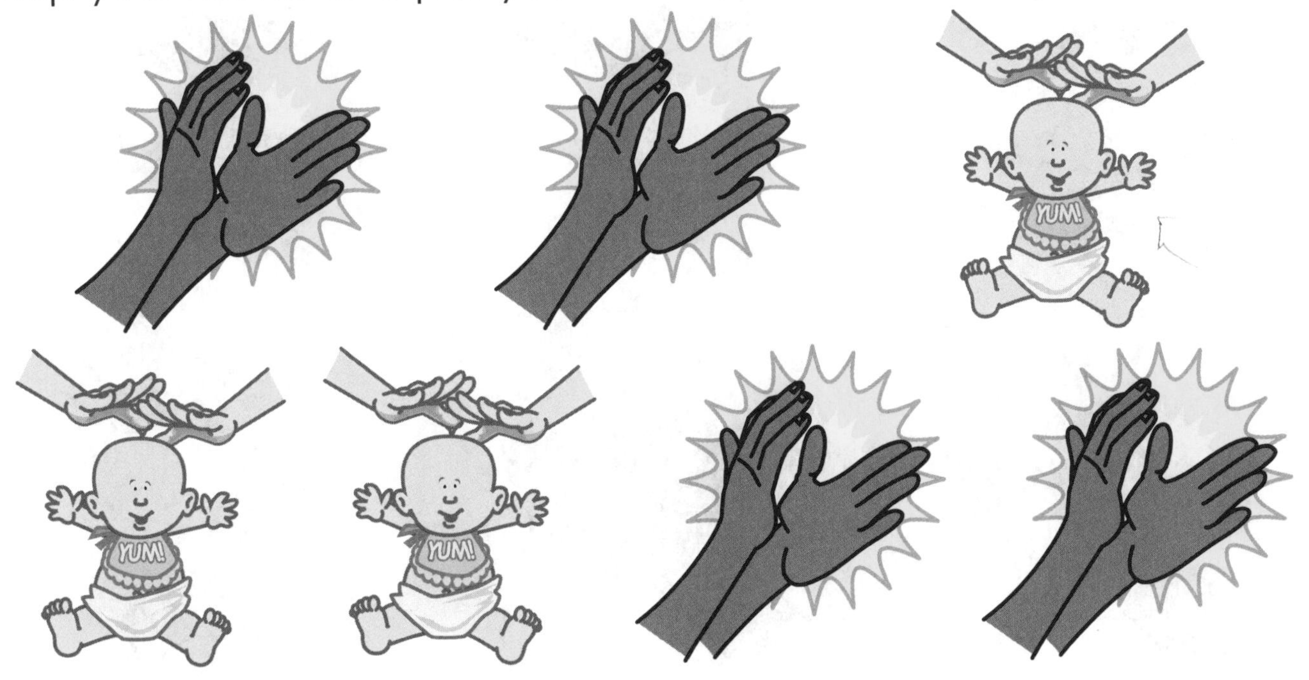

Name ______________________________

Clap Your Hands Again!

Clap your hands once, pat the top of your head two times, clap your hands two times, and then pause. Repeat this pattern three times.

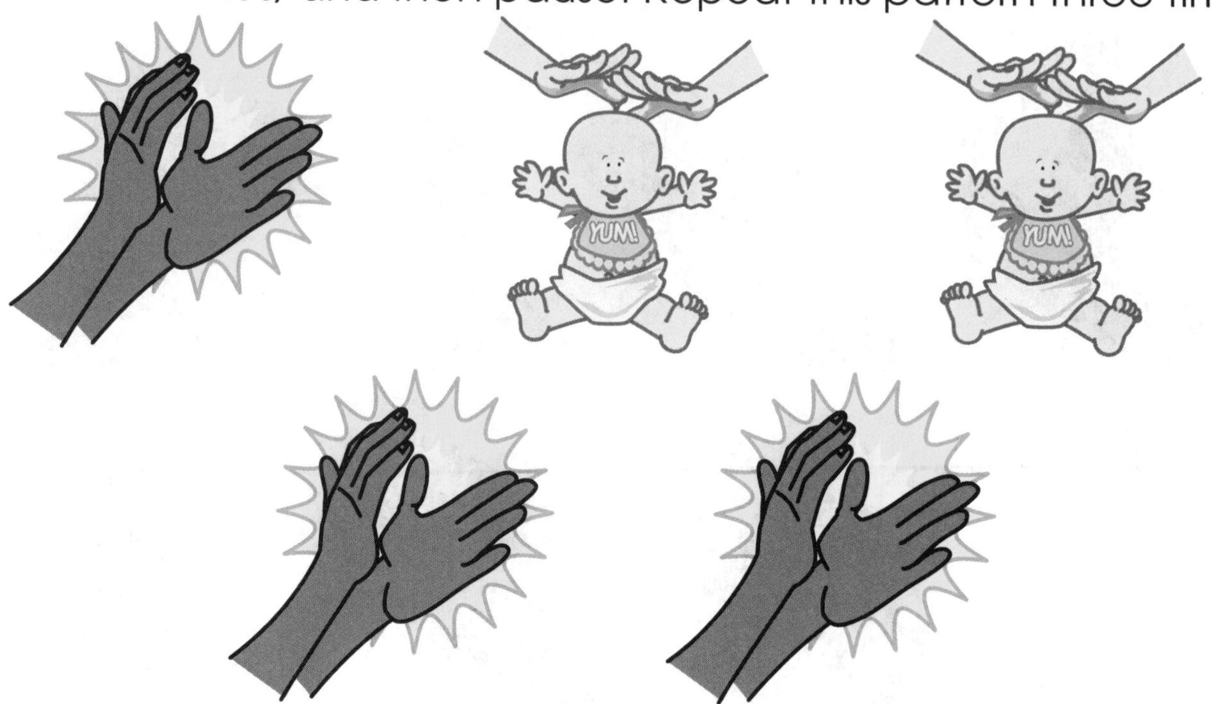

Pat your head and clap your hands as shown in the picture below.

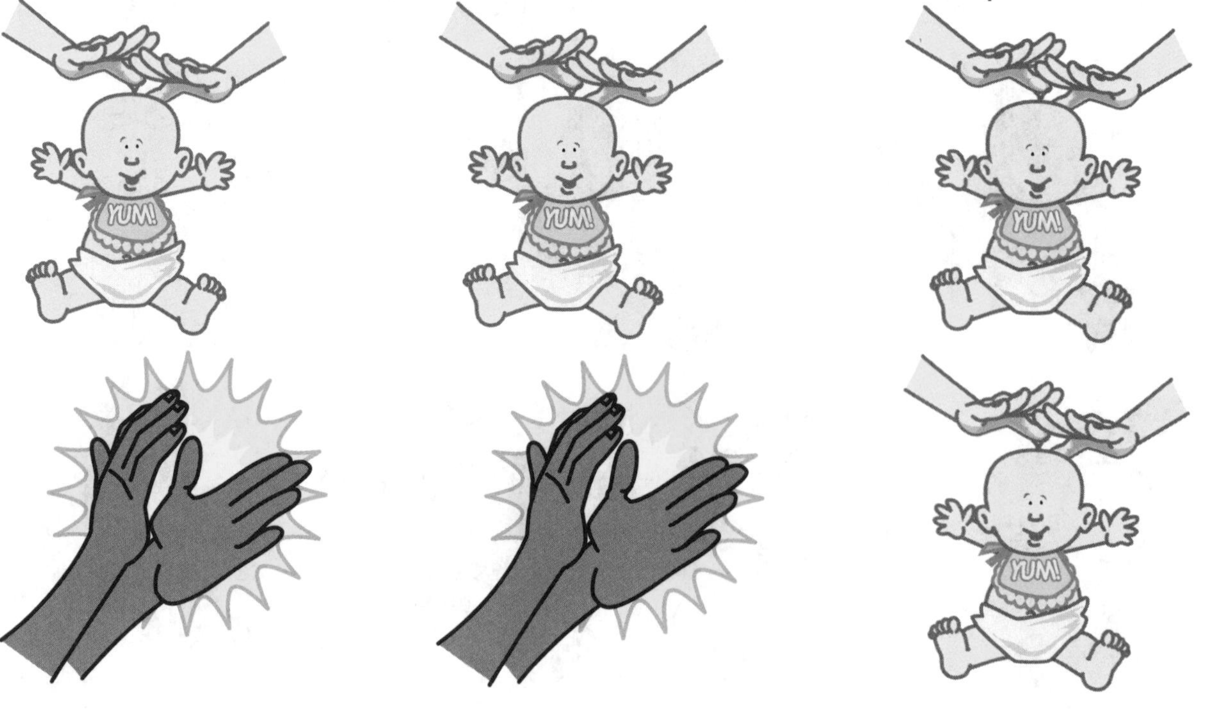

Name ____________________________

Copy That Pattern!

Use your blue crayon to make a copy of this pattern.

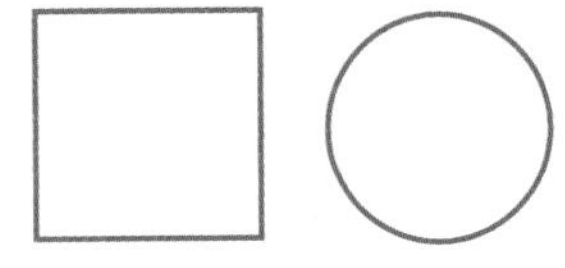 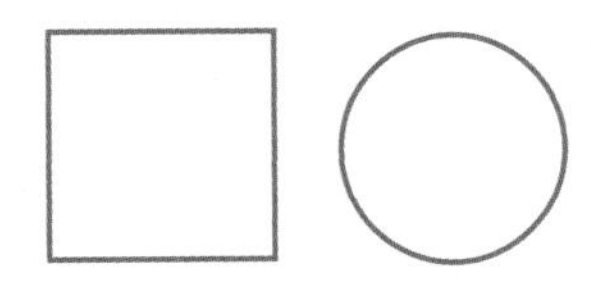 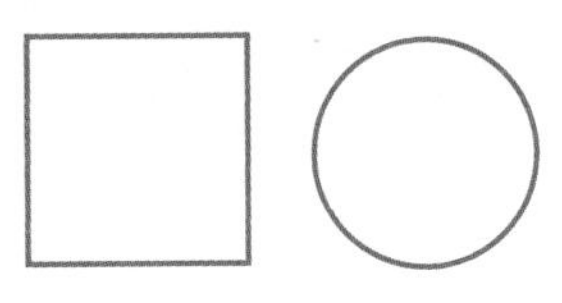

Use your red crayon to make a pattern of your own.

Use your purple crayon to copy your pattern backwards.

Name ______________________________

Copy Crazy!

Use your orange crayon to make a copy of this pattern.

  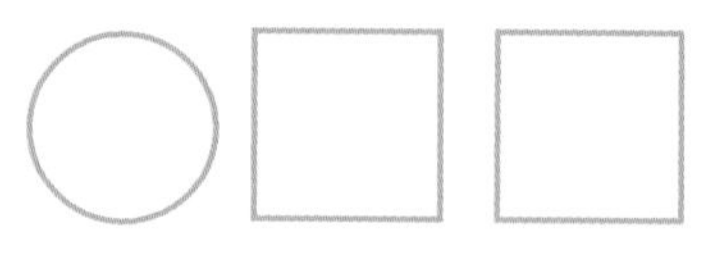

Use your yellow crayon to copy this pattern backwards.

Use your green crayon to make a pattern of your own.

Use your blue crayon to copy your pattern backwards.

Name ____________________

What's Next?

Use a pencil to continue each of the following patterns.
Then color your pattern.

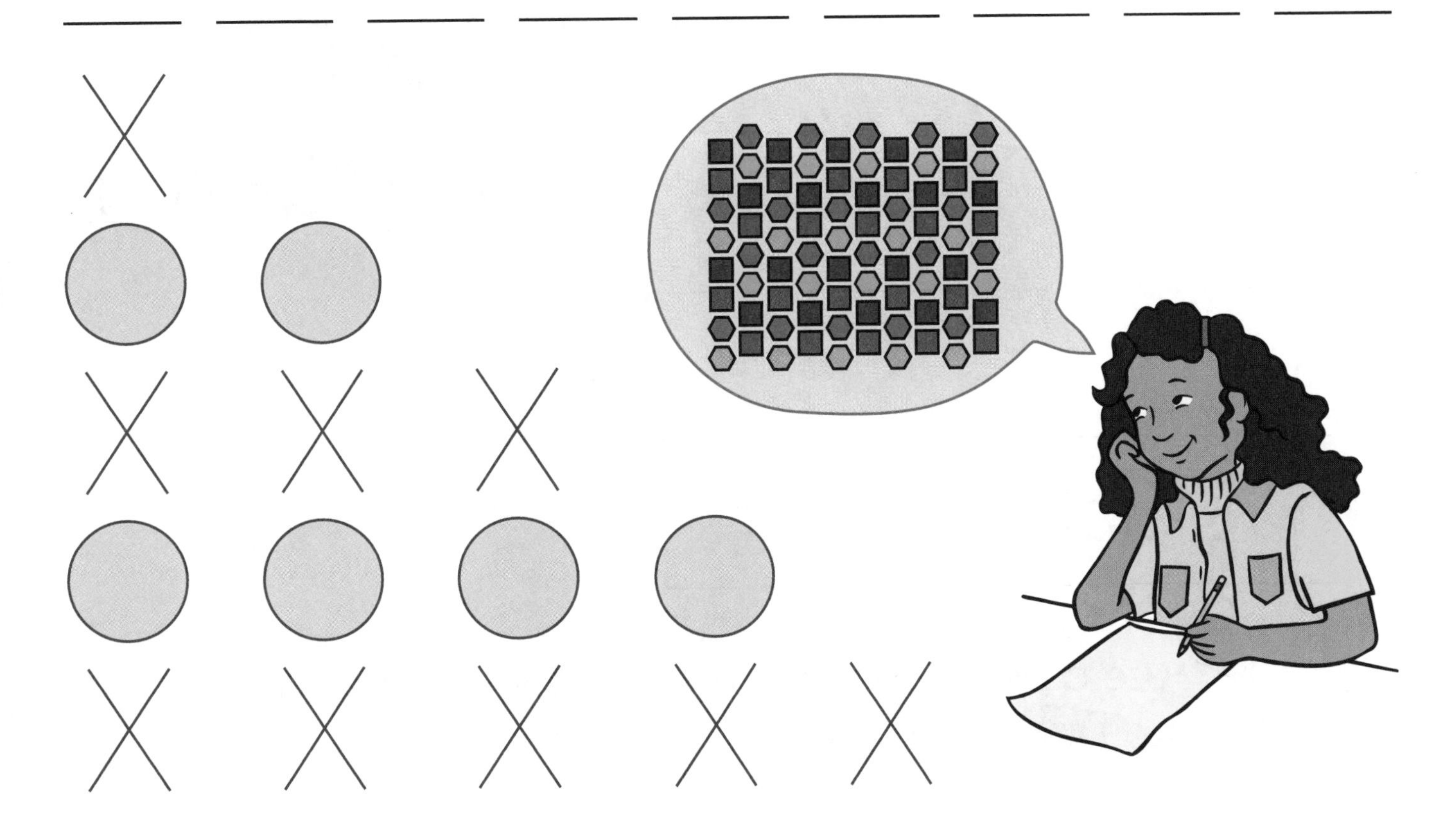

Name ______________________

Can You See the Pattern?

Use a pencil to continue the following pattern.

XXXXXX

XXXXX

XXXX

____

____

____

Use a pencil to make up your own pattern and draw it below. Then color your pattern.

Name ______________________

Inside, Above, Behind, and Beside

 Circle the object that is **inside** the toy box.

 Draw a square around the object that is **beside** the toy box.

Draw a triangle around the object that is **behind** the toy box.

 Draw a diamond around the object that is **above** the toy box.

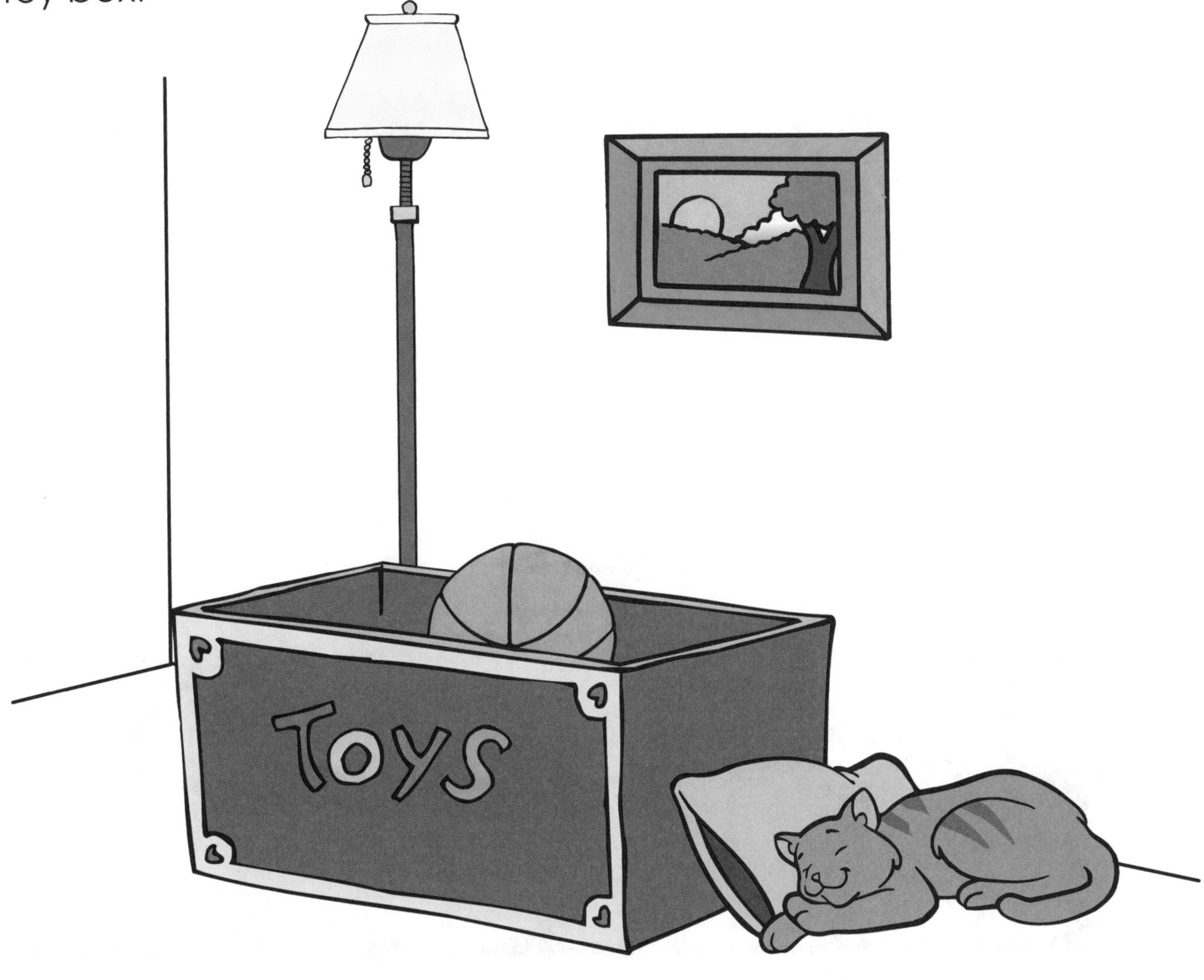

More Inside, Above, Behind, and Beside

Draw and color a flower **inside** the flower pot.

Draw and color a butterfly **above** the flower pot.

Draw and color a rainbow **behind** the flower pot.

Draw and color a dog sleeping **beside** the flower pot.

Name ___________________________

Monster Mash!

A two-ton monster came along and sat on each shape. What will they look like now?

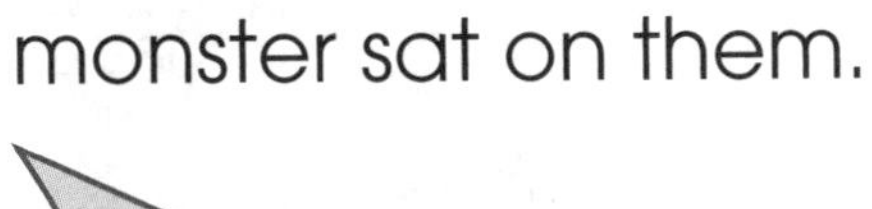

Draw a line to match each shape before and after the monster sat on them.

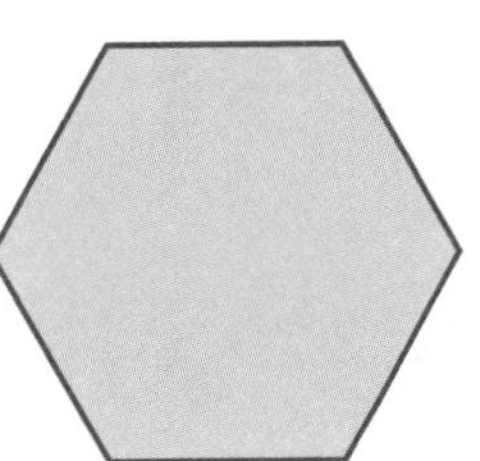

Elephant Bash!

Name ___________________________

Use your **red** crayon to draw a picture showing what each shape will look like after an elephant sits on the top of the shape.

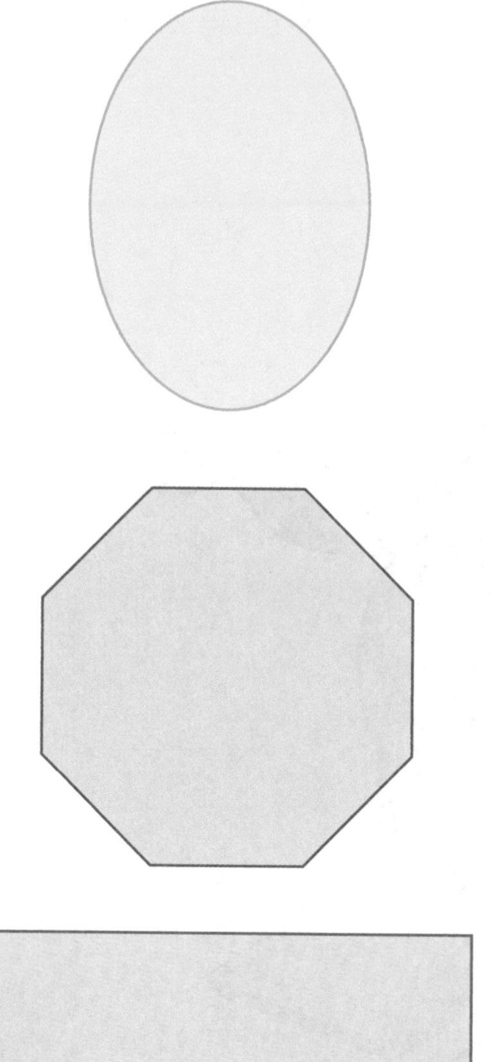

Name ______________________________

Copy Cat!

Use your crayons to make a copy of this design.

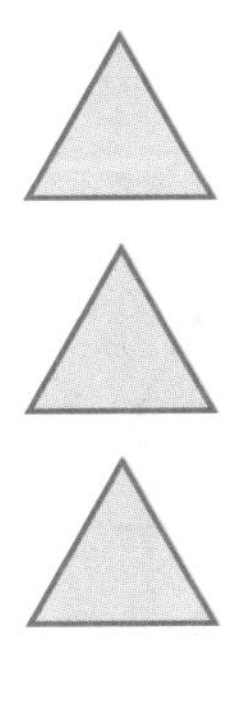

More Copy Cat!

Use your crayons to make a copy of this design.

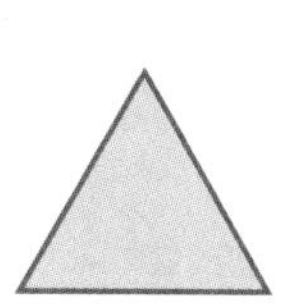

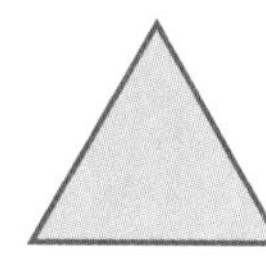

Name ______________________________

Up and Down—Left and Right

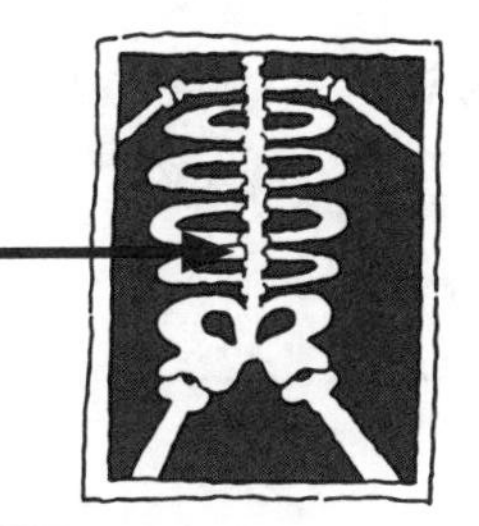

Vertical lines go up and down, like the vertebra in your spine.

Horizontal lines go left to right, like the horizon at sunset.

Circle the pictures below that show things that are **vertical**.

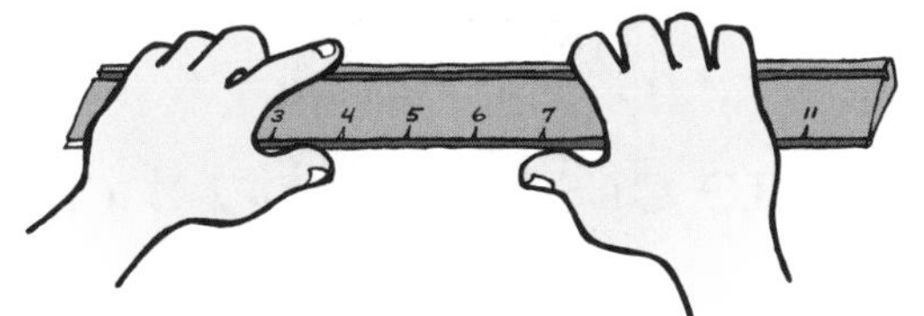

Circle the pictures below that show things that are **horizontal**.

Name ______________________________

Straight Up—Straight Across

Draw and color a picture of something that is **vertical**.

Draw and color a picture of something that is **horizontal**.

Name ______________________________

Measuring Up!

Circle the word that tells how much something **weighs**.

pound   inch   gallon

Circle the word that tells how **long** something is.

ounce   foot   quart

Circle the word that tells how much something **holds**.

ton   mile   gallon

Measuring Machines

Circle what you would use to measure the **weight** of the piece of cheese.

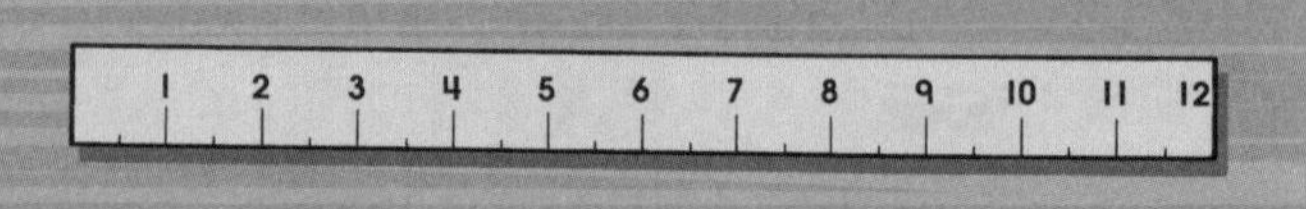

Circle what you would use to measure the **amount** of milk left in the milk bottle.

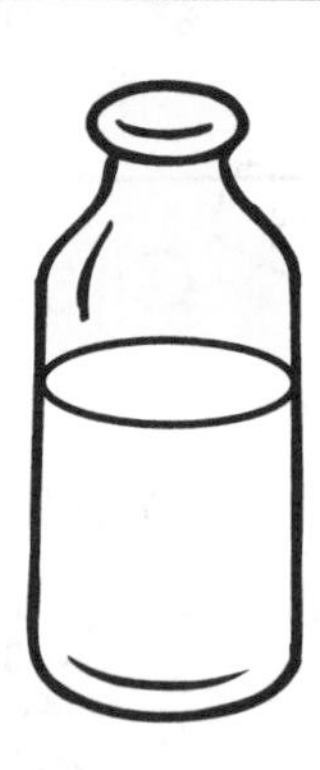

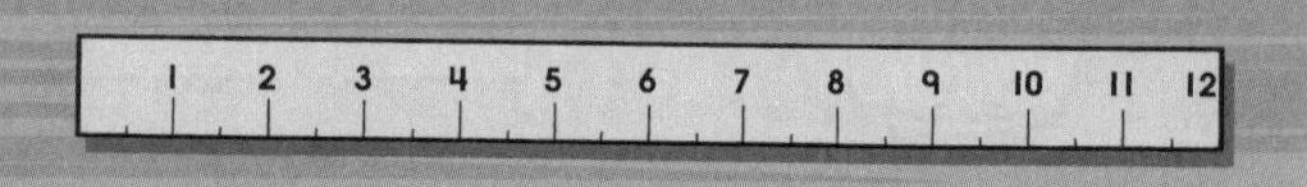

Circle what you would use to measure the **length** of the banana.

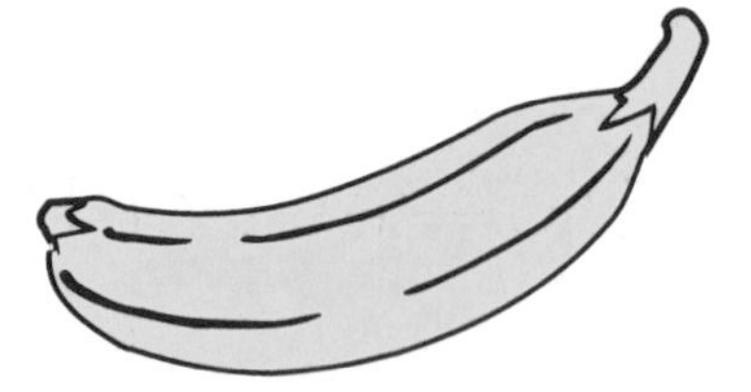

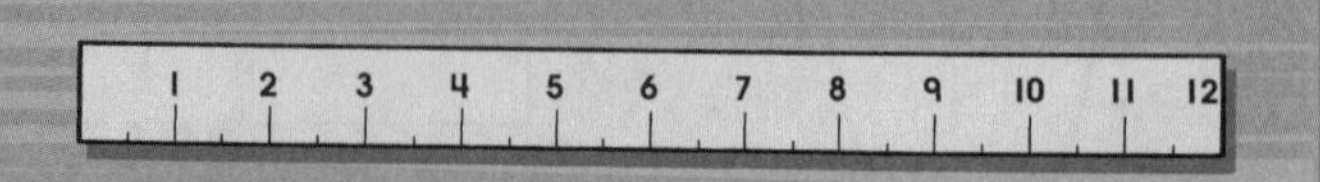

Name ___________________________

Full or Empty?

Circle with a red crayon each picture that shows something is **full**.

Circle with a blue crayon each picture that shows something is **empty**.

All or None?

Name ______________________

Draw and color a picture of something that is **full**.

Draw and color a picture of something that is **empty**.

Name ____________________

High Noon

Circle the things you usually do **before** lunch.

Circle the things you usually do **after** lunch.

Name ____________________

Night and Day

Circle the things you usually do at night.

Draw and color a picture of something you do **only** at night.

Name ______________________________

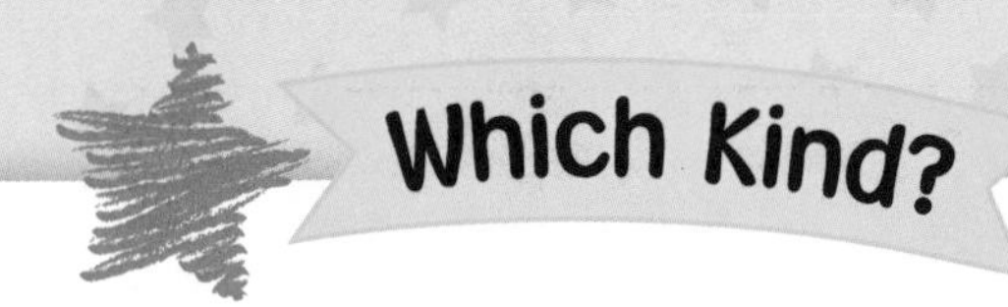

Which Kind?

Do you measure your **age** in years or in feet?

Circle your answer. years feet

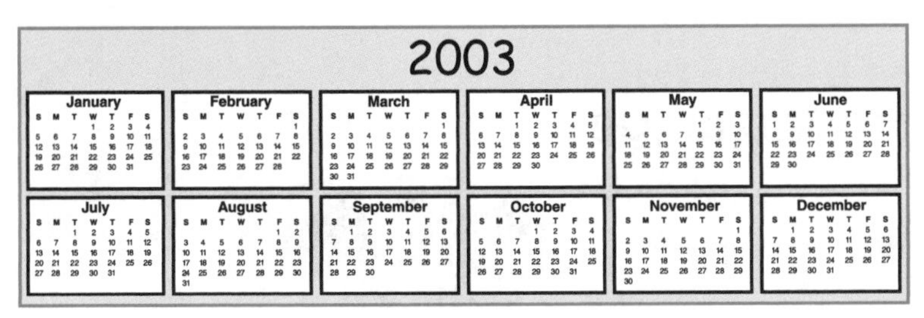

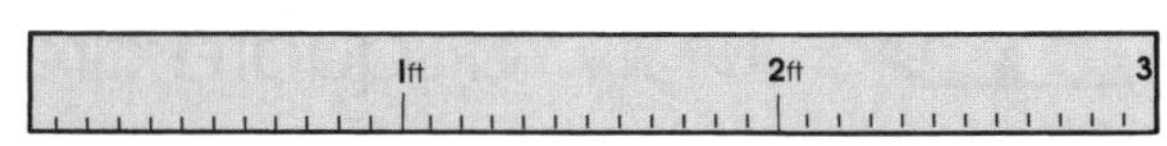

Do you measure your **height** in gallons or in inches?

Circle your answer. gallons inches

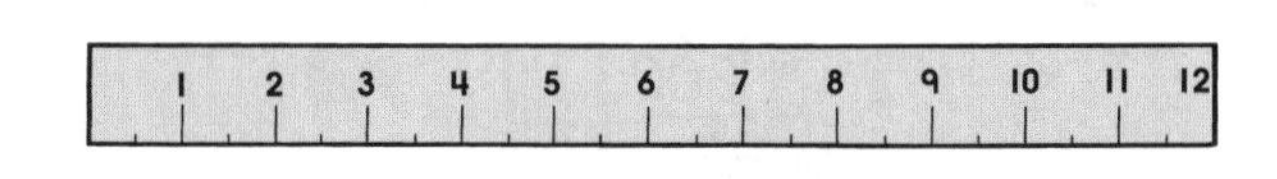

Do you measure your **weight** in weeks or in pounds?

Circle your answer. weeks pounds

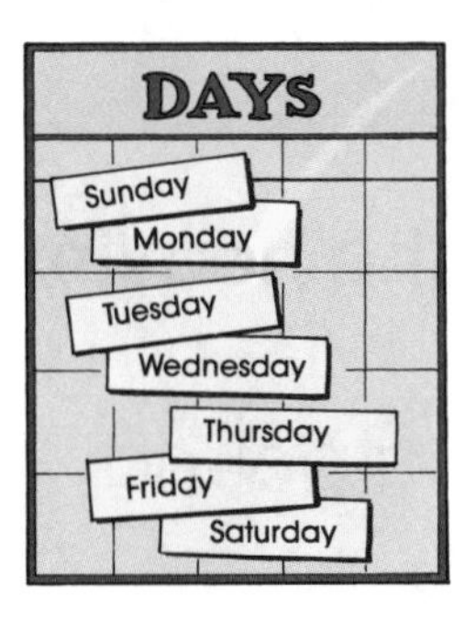

Smallest and Largest

Name ______________________________

Circle the **shortest**.

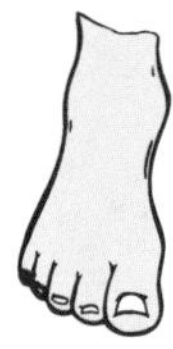 a foot  an inch  a mile

Draw a square around the **longest**.

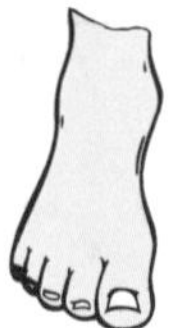 a foot  an inch  a mile

Circle the **shortest**.

a year  an hour  a day

Draw a square around the **longest**.

a year  an hour  a day

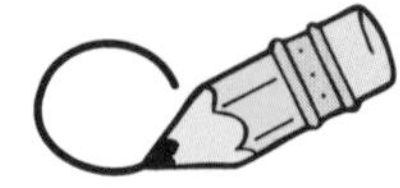

Circle the **lightest**.

 a ton  a pound  an ounce

Draw a square around the **heaviest**.

 a ton  a pound  an ounce

Name ______________________________

Matchmaker

Draw a line to connect objects that do the same kind of thing.

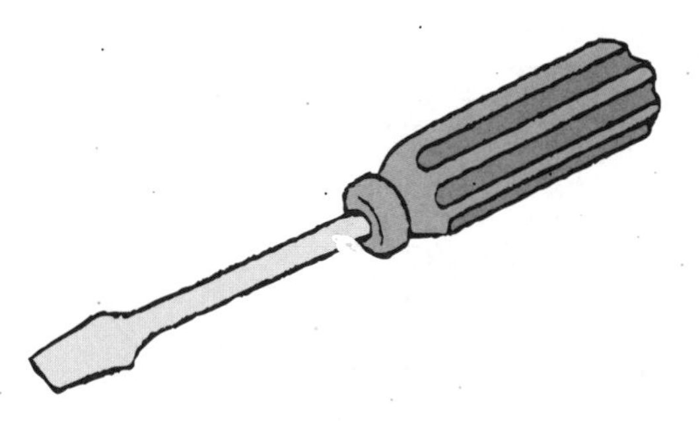

Matchmaker, Matchmaker

Draw a line to connect objects that do the same kind of thing.

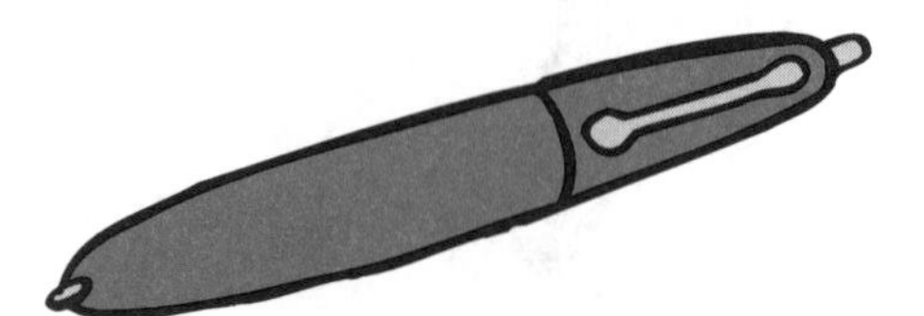

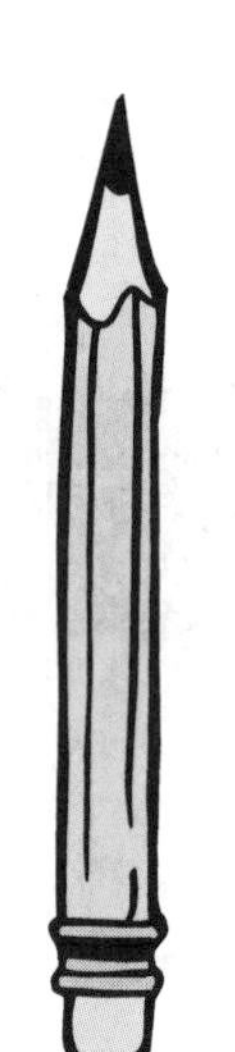

Name ____________________

Same But Different

How are a ball and a circle **similar** to each other?

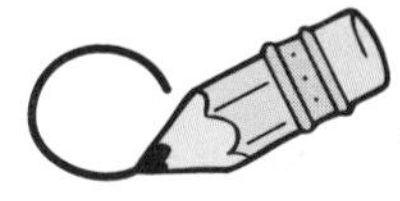 Circle one. both are square both are round

How are a ball and a circle **different** from each other?

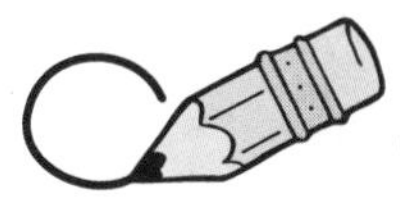 Circle one. both are flat one is flat and one is not

How are a square and a cube **similar** to each other?

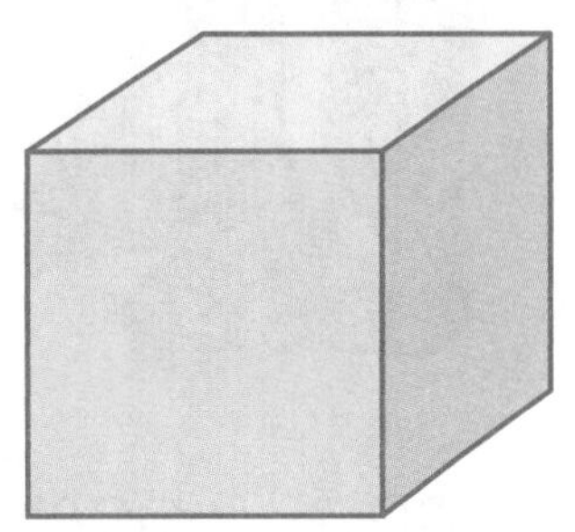

 Circle one. both are square both are round

How are a square and a cube **different** from each other?

 Circle one. both are flat one is flat and one is not

Name ______________________________

More Same But Different

Describe how an ice-cream cone and a pyramid are **similar**.

Circle one. both have "points" both are round

Describe how an ice-cream cone and a pyramid are **different**.

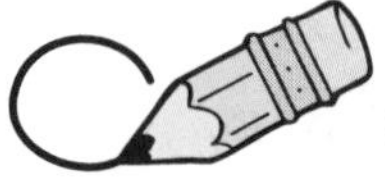

Circle one. one is round and one is square
both are square

Describe what makes these things **similar**.

Circle one. both are the same color
both come in twos

Describe how these things are **different**.

Circle one. both are different colors
both come in twos

Name ____________________

We Belong Together!

Look at the objects below.

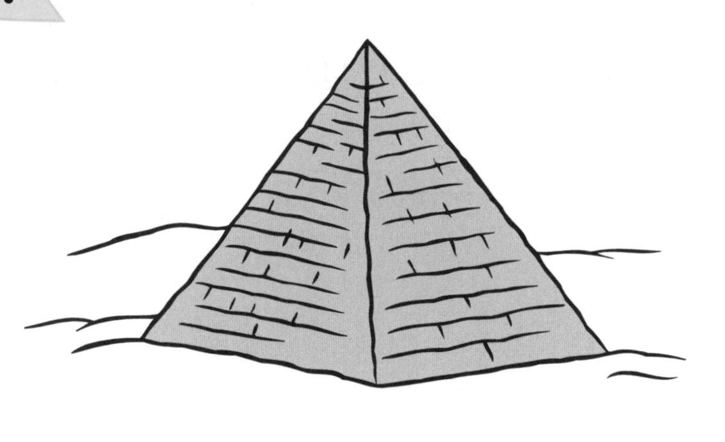

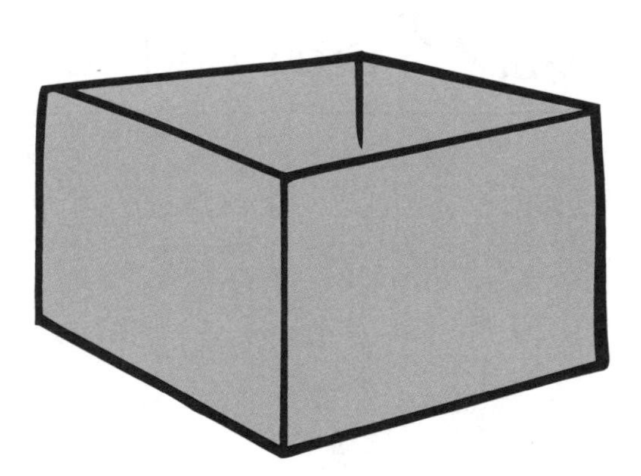

Which objects go together?

Draw a line to connect the two objects that belong together.

Name ____________________

We Have Something in Common!

Draw a line to connect two objects that have something in common.

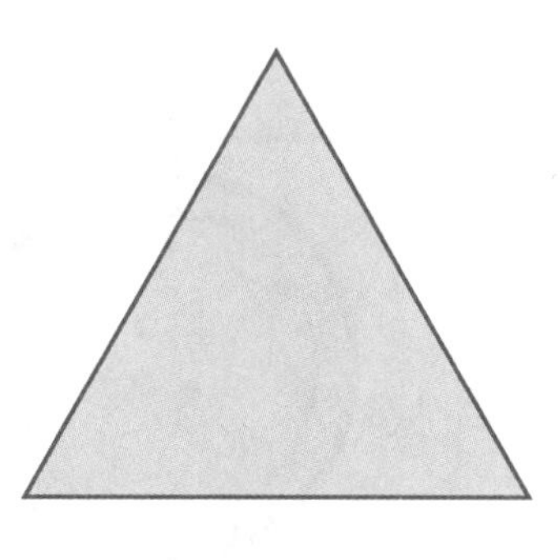

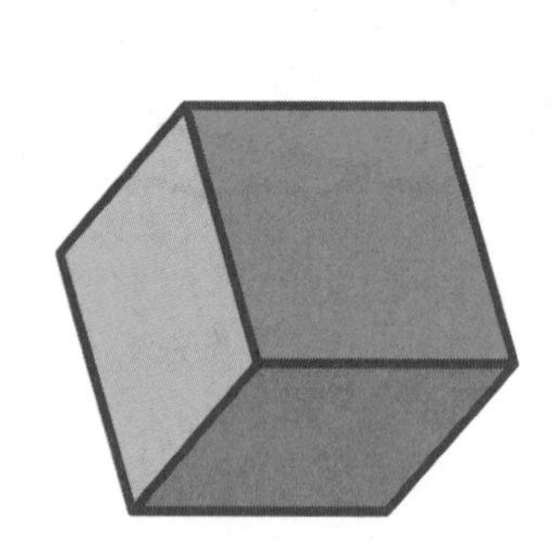

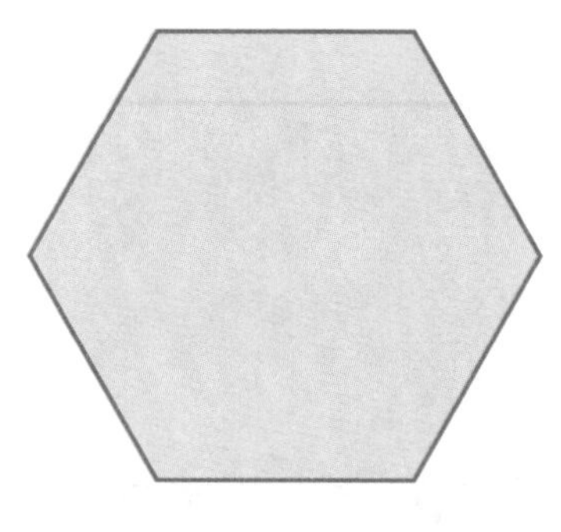

Draw and color two things that go together.

Name ____________________

Graph It!

Billy made a chart of all his stuffed animals.

Which animal does he have the **most** of?

Circle it with a red crayon.

Which animal does he have the **least** of?

Circle it with a blue crayon.

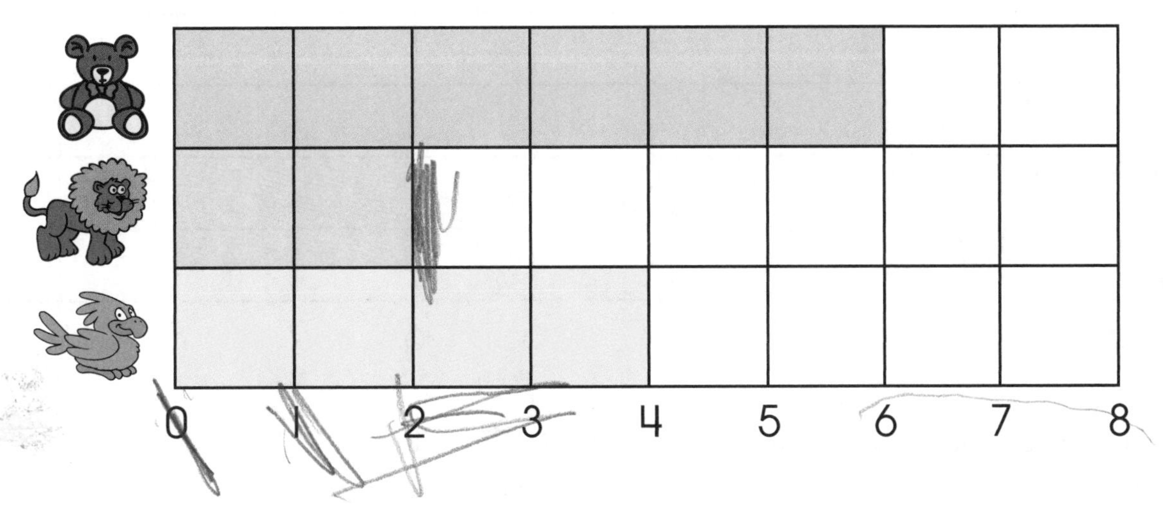

Take ten pennies and drop them on the floor.
Count how many heads and tails are showing.

Fill in the bar graph.

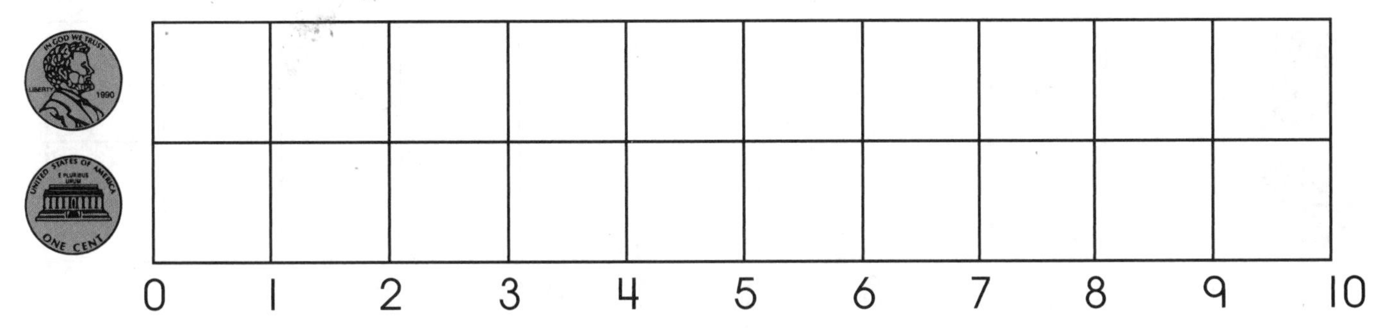

Name ______________________________

Amy made a chart of all of her money.

Which coin does she have the **most** of?

 Circle it with a green crayon.

Which coin does she have the **least** of?

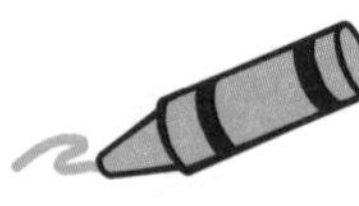 Circle it with an orange crayon.

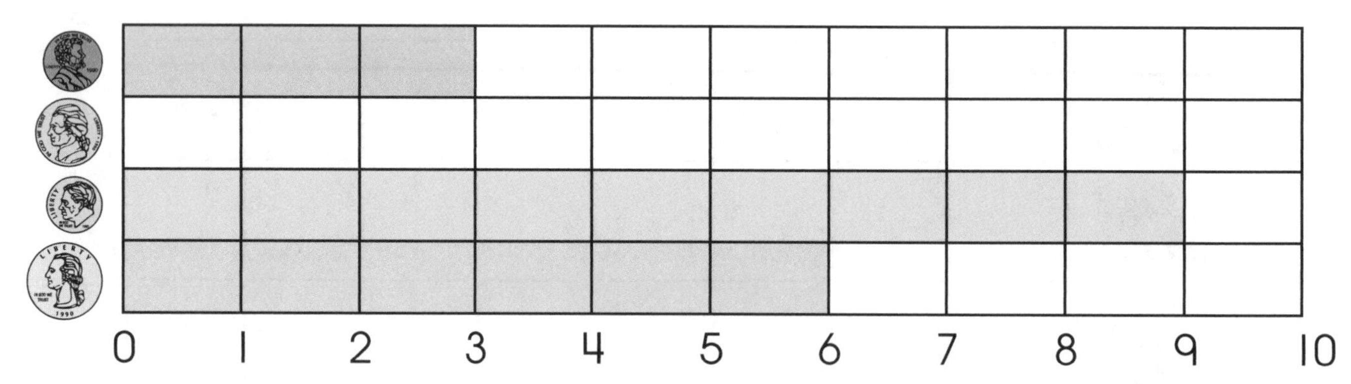

Take ten pennies and drop them on the floor again.
Count how many heads and tails are showing.

 Fill in the bar graph.

Repeat this three more times and see how the numbers change.

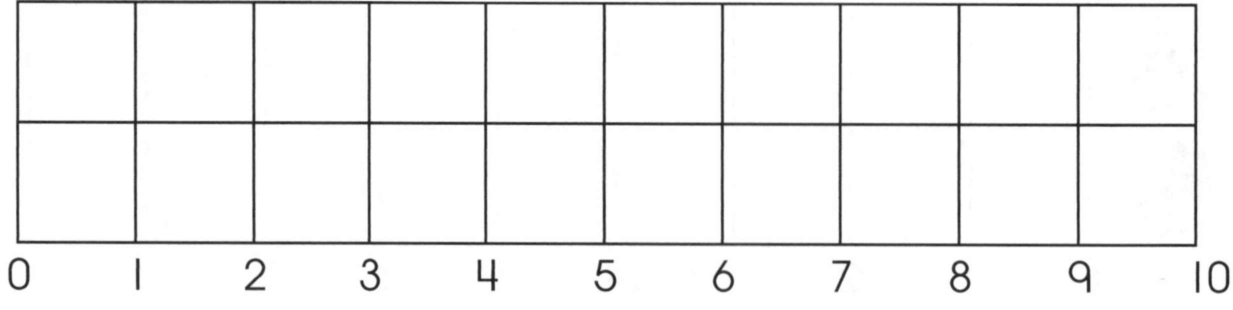

Half Full or Half Empty?

This cup is half full. The cup contains five ounces of juice. How much does the cup hold when it is full?

Circle your answer. 0 5 10 15 20 25

This pitcher holds 20 ounces of water. Half of the water is poured out. How many ounces are left?

Circle your answer. 0 5 10 15 20 25

Name ______________________________

This cup is full and contains 12 ounces of juice. After Jason drinks half of the juice, how many ounces will be left?

Circle your answer. 4 5 6 7 8 9 10

This pitcher is half full and contains 12 ounces of water. How much does the pitcher hold when it is full?

Circle your answer. 12 15 18 21 24 27

Name ______________________________

Cats, Dogs, and Birds, Oh My!

Sara and her friends decided they would make clothes for Sara's pets. Sara has one dog, one cat, and one parrot.

How many shoes should the girls make for all of the animals?

 Circle your answer.

4 6 8 10 12

How many hats should the girls make for all of the animals?

 Circle your answer. 0 1 2 3 4 5

How many earmuffs should the girls make for all of the animals?

 Circle your answer. 2 3 4 5 6 7

Name ______________________________

More Cats, Dogs, and Birds!

The girls had so much fun making clothes for Sara's pets that they decided to make clothes for Maria's pets. Maria has two dogs, one cat, and two lovebirds.

How many shoes should the girls make?

 Circle your answer.

6 8 10 12 14 16

How many hats should the girls make?

 Circle your answer. 1 2 3 4 5 6

How many earmuffs should the girls make?

 Circle your answer. 1 2 3 4 5 6

Name ________________________

Sally has one brother and two sisters.

How many girls are in the family?

 Circle your answer. 0 1 2 3 4 5

How many children are in the family?

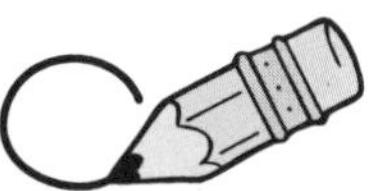 Circle your answer. 0 1 2 3 4 5

How many hands do the children have altogether?

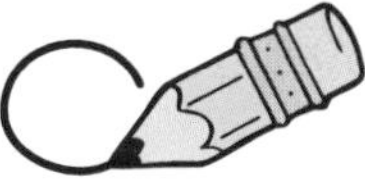 Circle your answer. 2 4 6 8 10

How many fingers do the children have altogether?

 Circle your answer. 10 20 30 40 50

Name ____________________

More Family Matters

James has two brothers and two sisters.

How many boys are in the family?

 Circle your answer. 0 1 2 3 4 5

How many children are in the family?

 Circle your answer. 0 1 2 3 4 5

How many hands do the children have altogether?

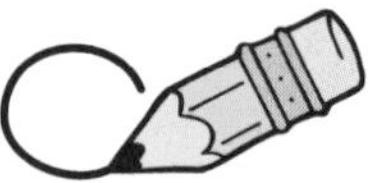 Circle your answer. 5 10 15 20 25

How many fingers do the children have altogether?

 Circle your answer. 30 40 50 60 70

Name ____________________

Balancing Act

For a scale to balance, there must be the same amount on both ends. This scale has 10 on each end, so it is in balance.

This scale is out of balance. It has 10 on the right end, but only 7 on the left end. How much should be put on the left end to make the scale balance?

Circle your answer. 0 1 2 3 4 5

This scale is also out of balance. It has 12 on the left end, but only 5 on the right end. How much should be put on the right end to make the scale balance?

Circle your answer. 5 6 7 8 9 10

Name ______________________

Keeping Things in Balance

For a scale to balance, there must be the same amount on both ends. This scale has 12 on each end, so it is in balance.

This scale is out of balance. It has 12 on the right end, but only 5 on the left end. How much should be put on the left end to make the scale balance?

 Circle your answer. 5 6 7 8 9 10

This scale is out of balance the other way. It has 15 on the left end, but only 10 on the right end. How much should be put on the right end to make the scale balance?

 Circle your answer. 5 6 7 8 9 10

Name ________________________

Going Around in Circles

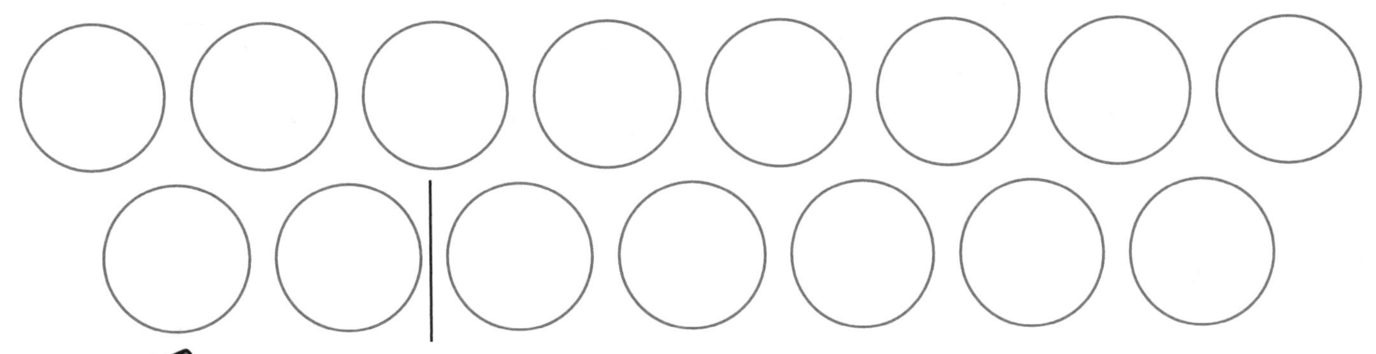

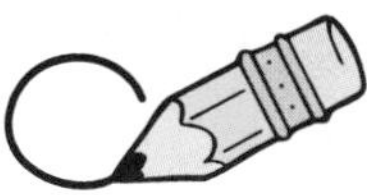 Color two circles. Use different colors.
How many circles are **not** colored?

 Circle your answer. 10 11 12 13 14 15

 Color three more circles. Use different colors.
How many circles are colored now?

Circle your answer. 5 6 7 8 9 10

How many circles are **not** colored?

Circle your answer. 5 6 7 8 9 10

 Color half of the remaining circles.
How many circles are colored now?

Circle your answer. 10 11 12 13 14 15

How many circles are **not** colored?

 Circle your answer. 5 6 7 8 9 10

Name ____________________

Going Around and Around in Circles

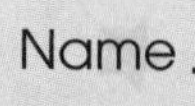

Color five circles. Use different colors.
How many circles are **not** colored?

Circle your answer. 0 5 10 15 20 25

Color five more circles. Use different colors.
How many circles are colored now?

Circle your answer. 0 5 10 15 20 25

How many circles are **not** colored?

Circle your answer. 0 5 10 15 20 25

Color half of the remaining circles. Use different colors.
How many circles are colored now?

Circle your answer. 0 5 10 15 20 25

How many circles are **not** colored?

Circle your answer. 0 5 10 15 20 25

Bigger Than—Smaller Than

Name ____________________

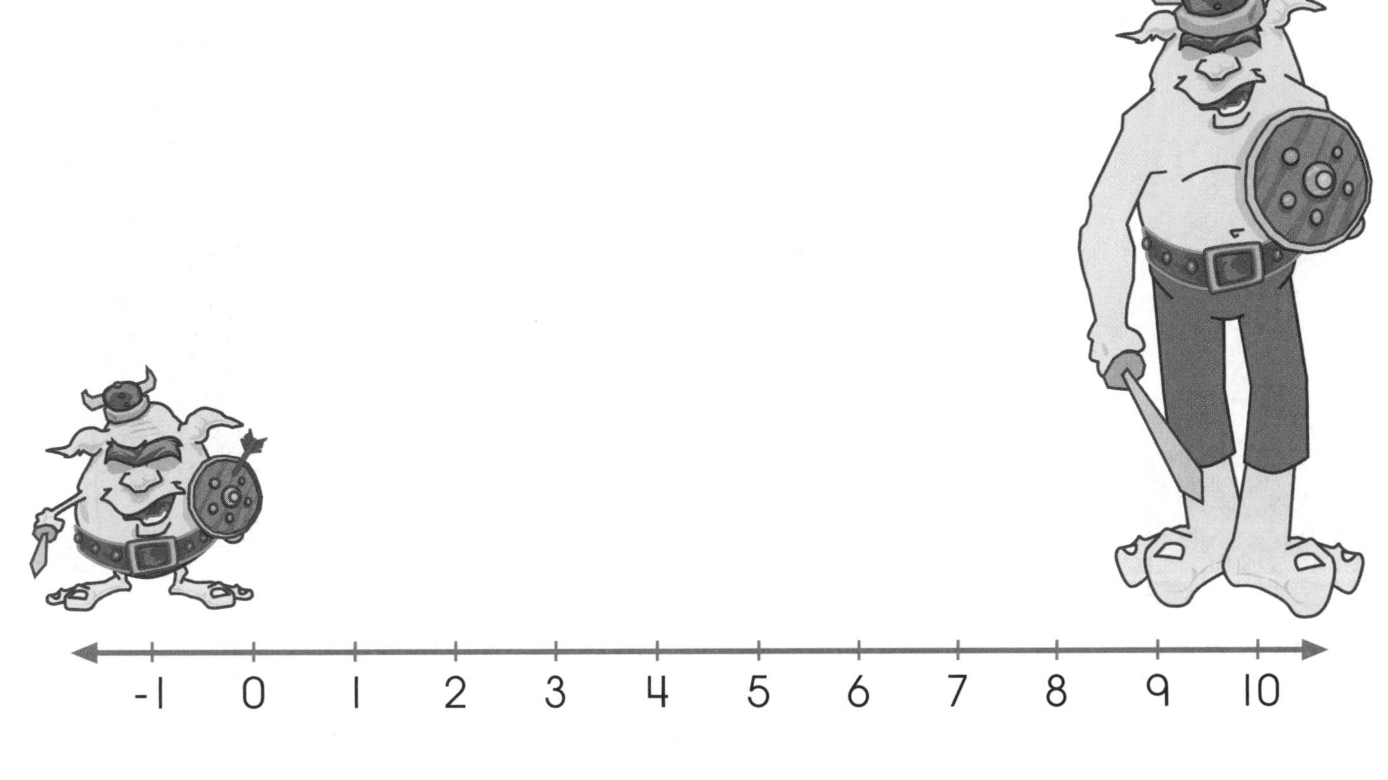

I am a number that is bigger than 5 and smaller than 7. What number am I?

 Circle your answer. 4 5 6 7 8 9

I am a number that is bigger than 4 and smaller than 9. What numbers can I be?

 Circle your answers. 4 5 6 7 8 9

Look at the number line above to help you answer this question: What number is in the middle of 0 and 10?

 Circle your answer. 4 5 6 7 8 9

Name ____________________

Bigger Than—Smaller Than Again

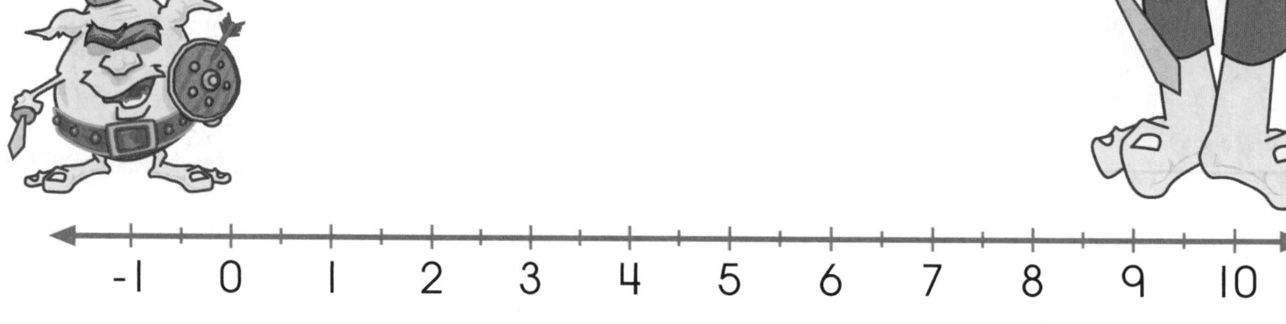

I am a number that is bigger than 4 and smaller than 5. What number am I?

Circle your answer. 3 $3\frac{1}{2}$ 4 $4\frac{1}{2}$ 5 $5\frac{1}{2}$ 6

I am a number that is smaller than 4. What numbers can I be?

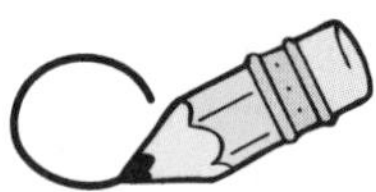

Circle your answer. -1 0 1 2 3 4 5

Look at the number line above to help you answer this question: What number is in the middle of 0 and 5?

Circle your answer. 2 $2\frac{1}{2}$ 3 $3\frac{1}{2}$ 4 $4\frac{1}{2}$ 5

Name ____________________

Cornering the Market

Circle all the shapes that have corners.

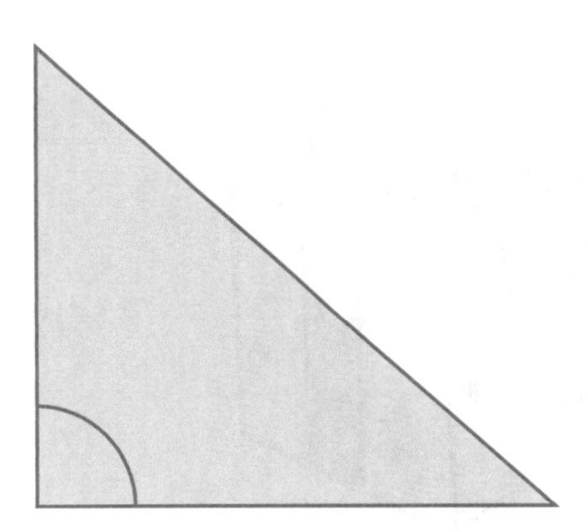

Draw and color a shape that has at least three corners.

Name ____________________

Round and Round

Circle all the shapes that have rounded edges.

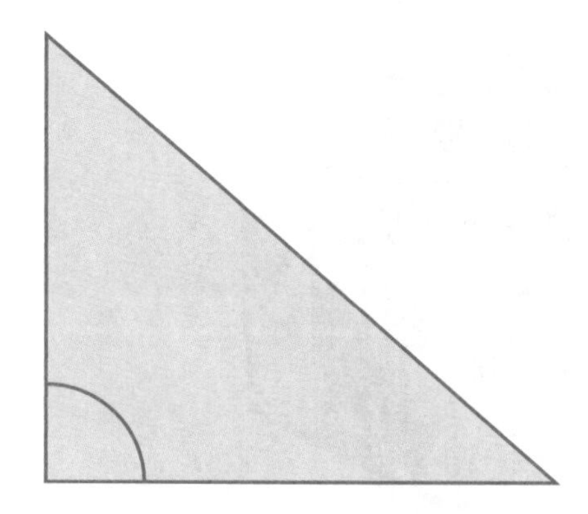

Draw and color a shape different from the ones above that has rounded edges.

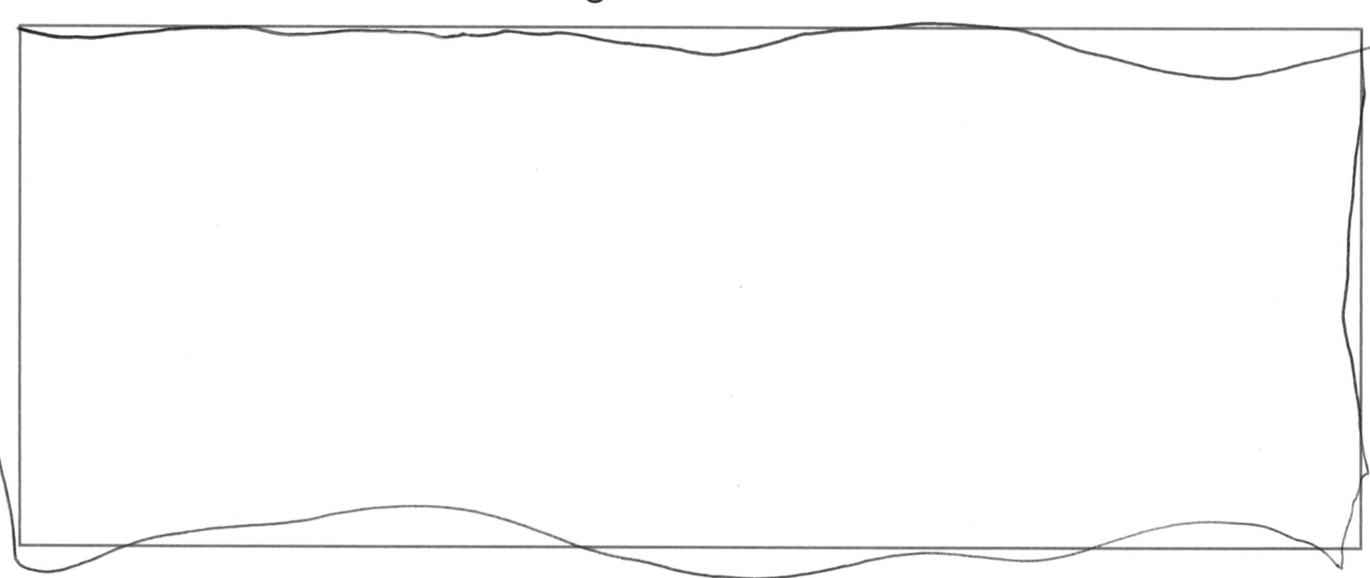

Name ____________________

Half and Half

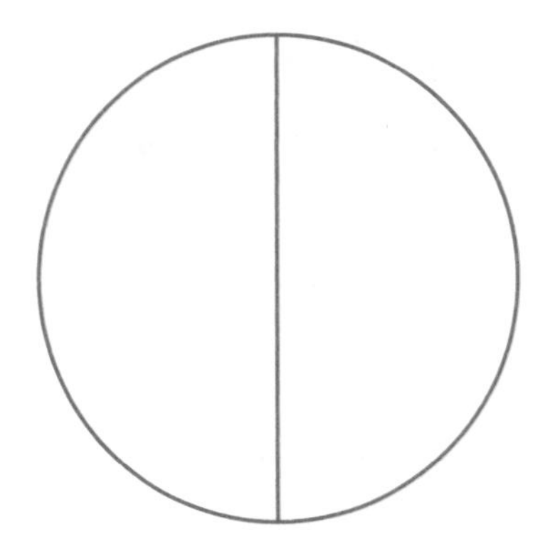
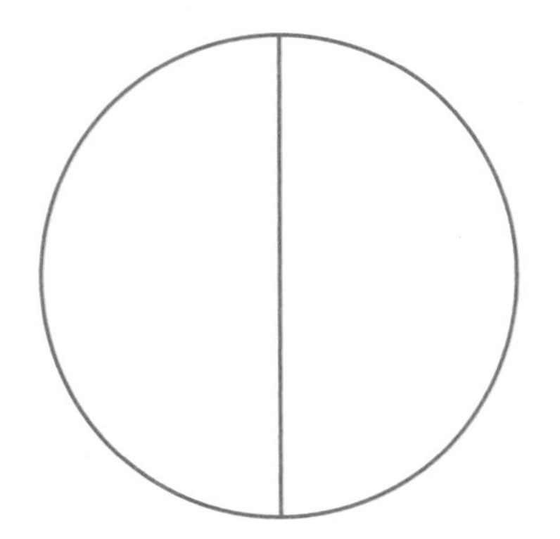
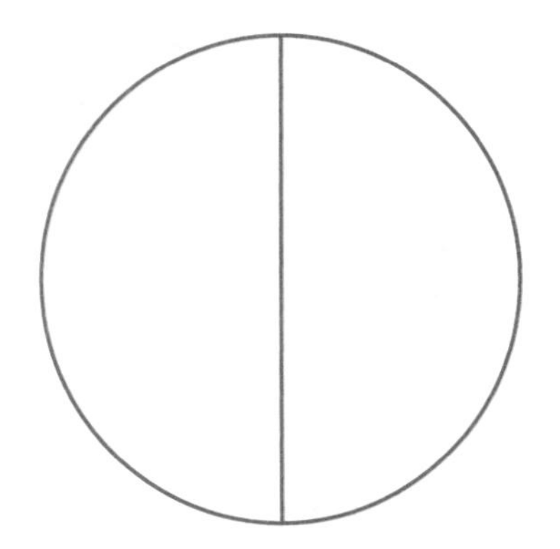

How many circles are there?

 Circle your answer. 1 2 3 4 5 6 7 8

Color half of each circle a different color.
How many different colors did you use?

 Circle your answer. 1 2 3 4 5 6 7 8

If you had used 10 colors, how many circles would there be?

 Circle your answer. 1 2 3 4 5 6 7 8

Draw three circles. 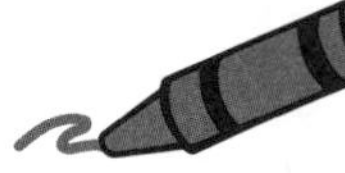 Color half of each one a different color.

Name ______________________

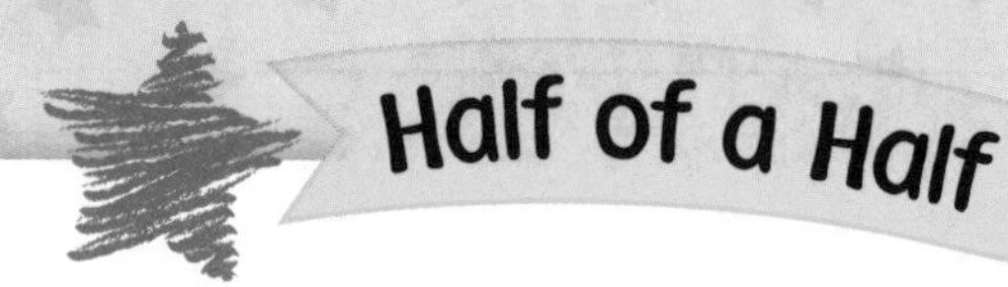

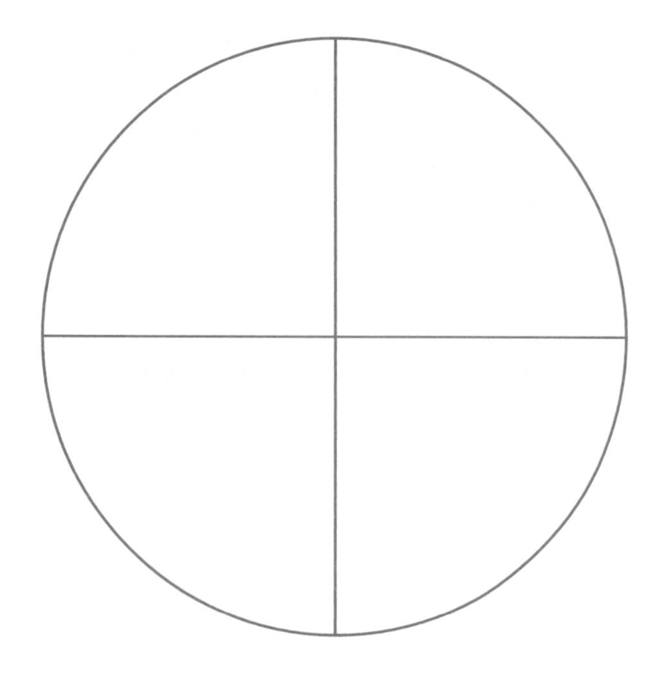

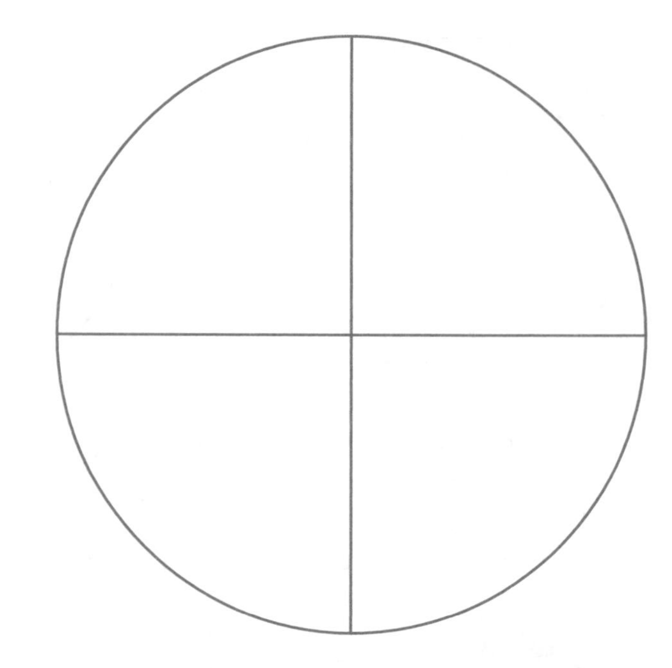

How many circles are there?

 Circle your answer. 1 2 3 4 5 6 7 8

Color each part of the circles a different color.
How many different colors did you use?

 Circle your answer. 1 2 3 4 5 6 7 8

If you had used 12 colors, how many circles would there be?

 Circle your answer. 1 2 3 4 5 6 7 8

Answer Key—Reading

Page 9
Children will answer the questions orally. Children's check marks on their favorite animals will vary.

Page 10
Children will answer the questions orally. Children's circled animals will vary.

Page 11
Children's pictures will vary.

Page 12
Children will answer the questions orally. Children will check either the cat or the dog.

Page 13

Children will answer the questions orally. Circled shoes will vary.

Page 14
Circle with red: pancakes, waffles, toast, eggs, coffee. Circle with blue: orange juice, milk, glasses with ice cubes. Children will answer the question orally.

Page 15
Circle bicycle, airplane, rabbit, go-carts. Draw an **X** on walkers and snail.

Page 16
Children will answer what is yellow and what is orange. Children will color the picture with appropriate colors for the fruit and vegetables.

Page 17

Children will answer questions orally. Circled ponies will vary.

Page 18

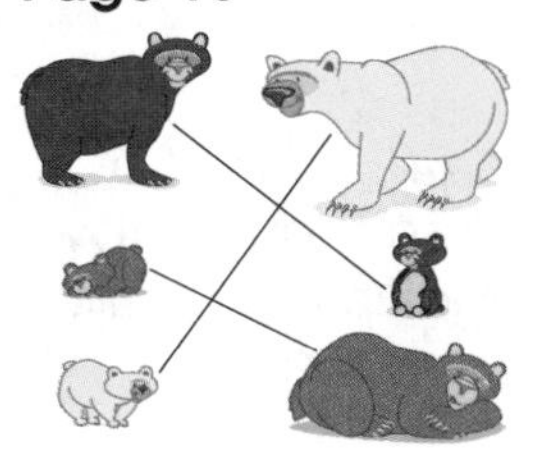

Children will answer the questions orally.

Page 19

Children will answer the question orally.

Page 20

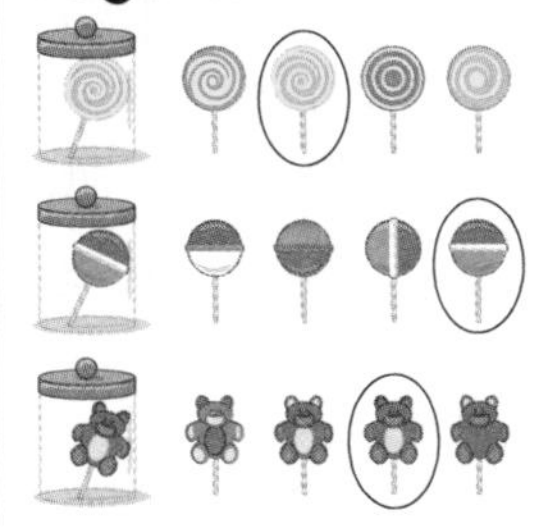

Children will answer the question orally.

Page 21
Color green the bird in the water. Color yellow the bird in the inner tube. Color red the bird under the umbrella. Color blue the bird by the rocks.

Page 22

Page 23

Page 24
Children should color yellow the rabbit, teddy bear, feather, and pillow.

Page 25

Page 26
Draw an **X** on: candy, slippers, shovel, ice-cream cone.

Page 27
Circle eyes, smile, nose in Row 1; circle bed, pillow, pajamas in Row 2; circle duck, porpoise, platypus in Row 3; circle mittens, hat, coat in Row 4.

Page 28
Draw an **X** on: panda, moose, beaver.

Page 29
Circle the pumpkin and Santa Claus cupcakes.

Page 30
Children should circle 5 of the following: nose, man, dog, newspaper, hair, and ears.

Page 31
Circle kangaroo in Row 1; circle bed in Row 2; circle bananas in Row 3. Children's stories and pictures will vary.

Page 32
Children will answer the questions orally.

Page 33

Page 34
Circle Jamal, put an **X** on Jamie, put a check mark on Jack. Children will answer the question orally.

Page 35
Children will answer the questions orally. Circle the jacket.

Page 36

Page 37

Page 38

Page 39
Color the cow behind the haystack brown, the middle cow blue, and the one at the bottom black and pink.

Page 40
Circle light bulb, man in scuba outfit, chicken, cat on grill, flying fish.

Page 41
Circle pillow in Row 1, tack in Row 2, banana in Row 3, pickle in Row 4.

Page 42
Circle blueberries in Row 1, slippers in Row 2, brownie in Row 3, ape in Row 4.

Page 43
Color ice-cream cone in Row 1, giraffe in Row 2, stove in Row 3, gems in Row 4.

Page 44
Color suitcase in Row 1, kid with bubble gum in Row 2, window in Row 3, whale in Row 4.

Page 45
Color the following pink: cotton candy, flamingo, and rose.

Page 46
Ben's sister is Crystal.

Page 47
Tim should pick the turtle with squares on its back. Answers will vary.

Page 48
Children should check the second picture.

Page 49
Children should check the last picture.

Page 50
Children should check the last picture.

Page 52
Children should draw and color the plum.

Page 54
Children should draw and color the chocolate donut with sprinkles.

Page 55
Children should draw a check mark on the first picture.

Page 56
Children should draw a check mark on the second picture.

Page 57
Children should draw a check mark on the last picture.

Page 58

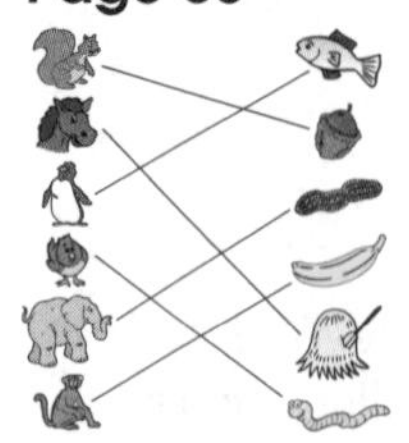

Page 59
Draw an **X** on the soccer ball, flowers, mailbox, shovel, pumpkins, swing, telephone. Pictures will vary.

Page 60
Draw an **X** on the fan, ball, wheel, golf club, bike, lawn mower, Thesaurus. Pictures will vary.

Page 61
Draw an **X** on the rattle, soda, drumstick, watermelon, soap.

Page 62
Children should circle the first picture. Answers will vary.

Page 63
Children should circle the second picture.

Page 64
Children should circle the second picture.

Page 65
Children should circle the second picture.

Page 66
Children should circle the first picture.

Answer Key—Writing

Page 67
Pictures for D and F will vary.

Page 68
Pictures for P and R will vary.

Page 69
Children will trace *A, and, away.*

Page 70
Children should circle: am, Are, ate, at, and, ate, all, Are, am

Page 71
Children should color the silly monster blue. Children should color the big blue monster's brother black and brown.

Page 72
Children should circle: Carmen, can, come, Carmen, came

Page 73
Children should circle: dogs, diving board, dive, deep end, duck, dolphin, dinosaur, and drip.

Page 74
Children's eggs will vary.

Page 75
Children will find and circle 4 funny 4's.

Page 76
Children's answers will vary. Children's pictures will vary.

Page 77
Heart, hand, hamster, and honey

Page 78
Children's pictures will vary.

Page 79
Children's pictures will vary.

Page 80
Children will circle the picture of the kite. Children's pictures will vary.

Page 81
Children will circle the picture of the lollipop.

Page 82
Children should color red the mouse, mirror, milk, mermaid, and man.

Page 83
Children will draw a nose, nail, neck, and necklace on the appropriate pictures.

Page 84
Children's pictures will vary.

Page 85
Children's stories and pictures will vary.

Page 86
Children's pictures will vary.

Page 87

Page 88

Children's stories will vary.

Page 89

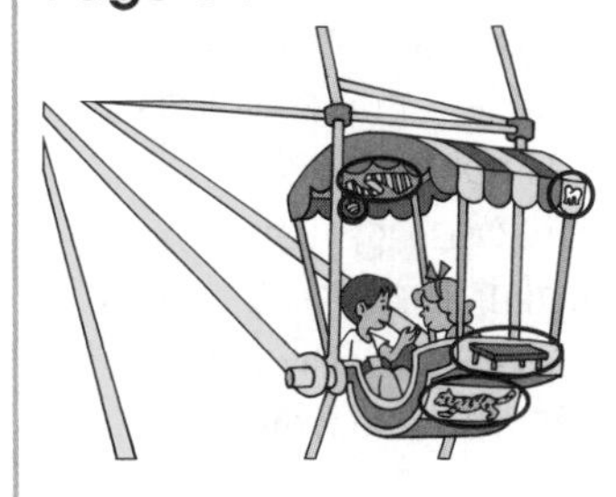

Children's stories will vary.

Page 91

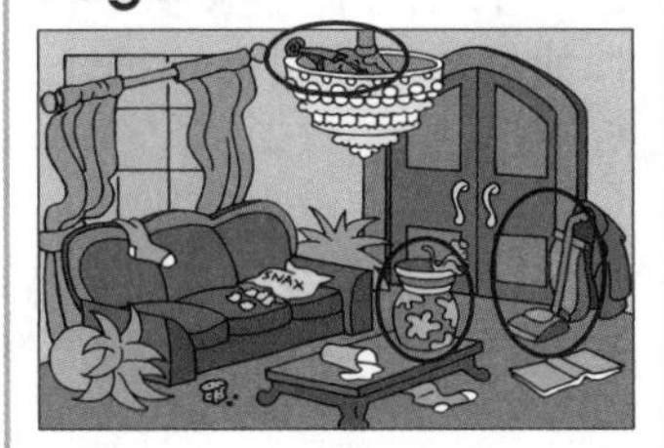

Page 92
Children should answer the waffle, the wheel, the walnut, the worm, and the whale.

Page 93
Children's pictures will vary.

Page 94
Children should color the X's green, the Y's yellow, and the Z's purple. Children should color the other zebra black and white.

Page 95

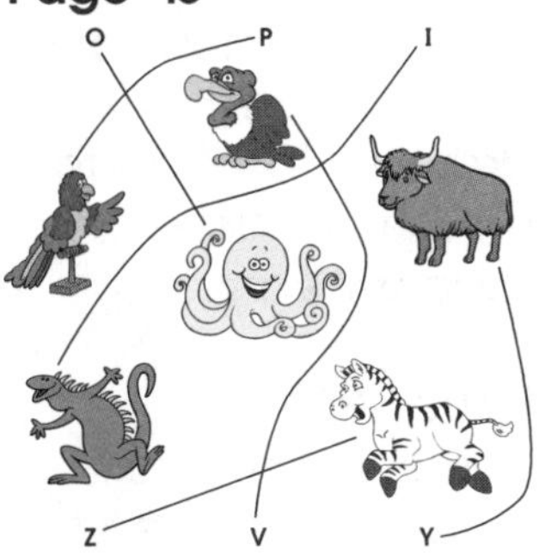

Page 96
Children should write H, E, X, U, L, K, O, D, C, R, Y, and B
Children's answers will vary.

Page 97
The balloons should have C, L, O, W, N written on each one. Children's stories will vary.

Page 98
Children's pictures will vary. Children's stories will vary.

Page 99

Page 100
Children's stories will vary.

Page 101
Children will color the eye and add eyelashes. Answers will vary for nose and ear. Children will draw teeth inside the mouth. Pictures of a face will vary.

Page 102
Children's answers will vary. Children's pictures will vary.

Page 103
Children's pictures will vary. Children's sentences will vary.

Page 104
A photo. Children's answers will vary.

Page 105
Pizza. Children's answers will vary.

Page 106
Ketchup. Children's answers will vary.

Page 107
Children will write I love you Mom. Children will write Dad I love you.

Page 108
Children will write this message: Hunters dream under stars.

Page 109
Children will trace lines moving from left to right.

Page 110
Children will draw a path with their crayons.

Page 111
Children should circle: green grass, chirping birds, blooming flowers, light rain, and green leaves. Children's stories will vary.

Page 112
Children should circle: big puddles, soggy worms, wet hair, people hurrying, and yellow raincoat. Children's words in the empty raindrop will vary. Children's answers will vary.

Page 113

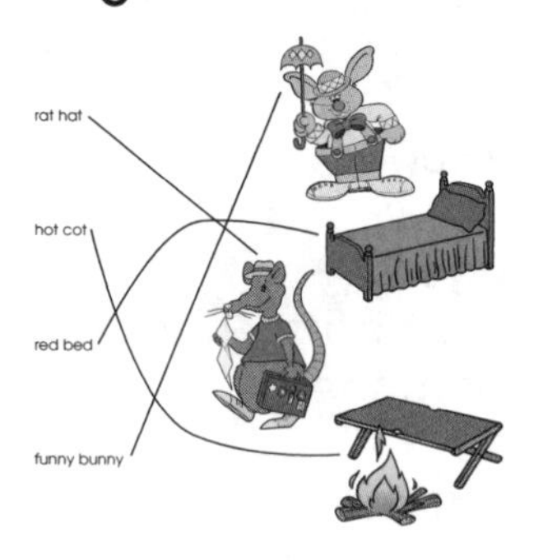

Page 114
Children's words will vary. Children's pictures will vary.

Page 115

Page 116

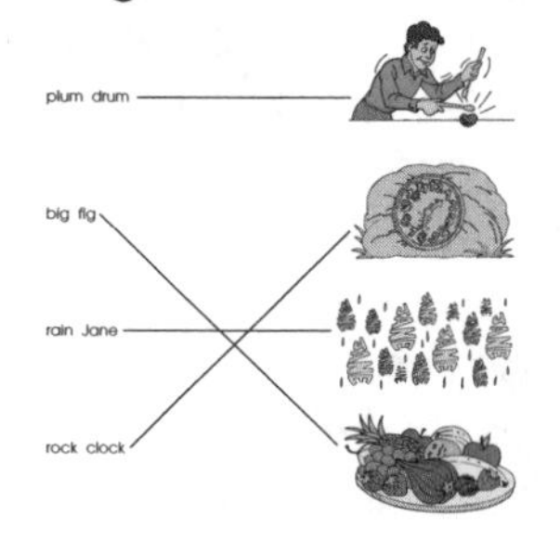

Page 117
Children's pictures will vary.

Page 118
Children's pictures will vary.

Page 119
Children's sentences will vary. Children's pictures will vary.

Page 120
Children's answers will vary. Children's pictures will vary.

Page 122
Children's recipes will vary. Children's pictures will vary.

Page 123
Children's answers will vary. Children's stories and pictures will vary.

Page 124
Children's lists will vary.

Answer Key—Math

Page 125

Page 126

Page 127

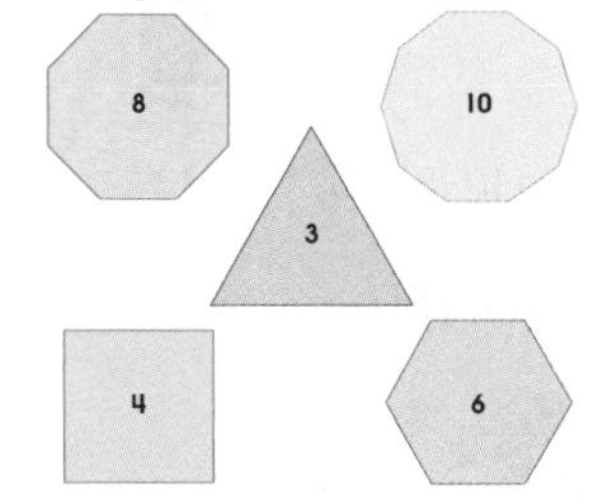

Page 128
6 sheep
5 cows
more sheep
12 legs
2 cows

Page 129
4 rows of cars
2 cookies

Page 130
5 coins
4 groups of 5

Page 131
0 dollars
20 dollars
0 nickels

Page 132
5 dollars
0

Page 133
1 piece of 3

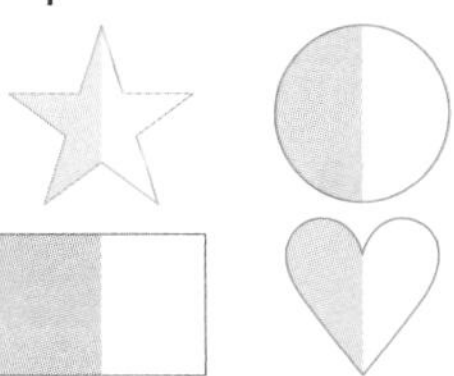

Page 134
4 pieces
3 circles are not colored
5 circles are not colored
$2\frac{1}{2}$ circles are not colored

Page 135
10 shoes
1 child is in the pool
2 children went home

Page 136
9 people
7 people

Page 139

Patterns will vary.

Page 140

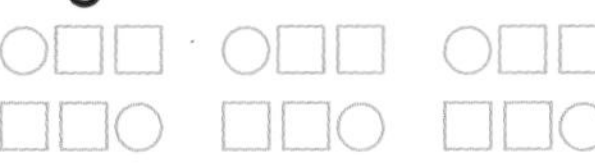

Patterns will vary.

Page 141

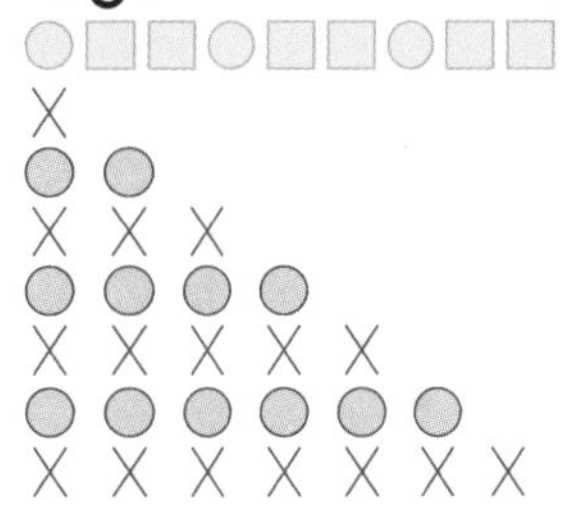

Page 142

XXXXXX
XXXXX
XXXX
XXX
XX
X

Patterns will vary.

Page 143

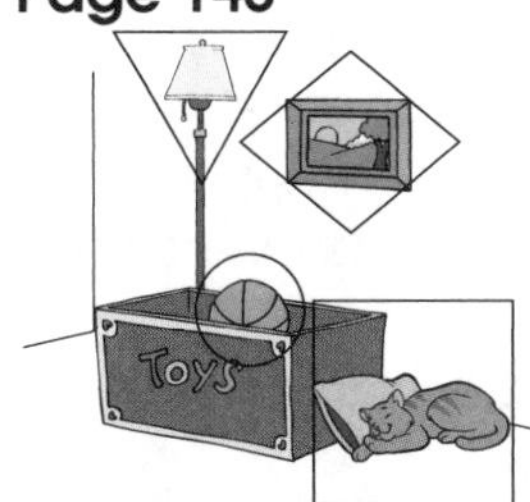

Page 144

Page 145

Page 146
Pictures will vary but should resemble what an oval, octagon, and rectangle will look like squashed.

Page 147

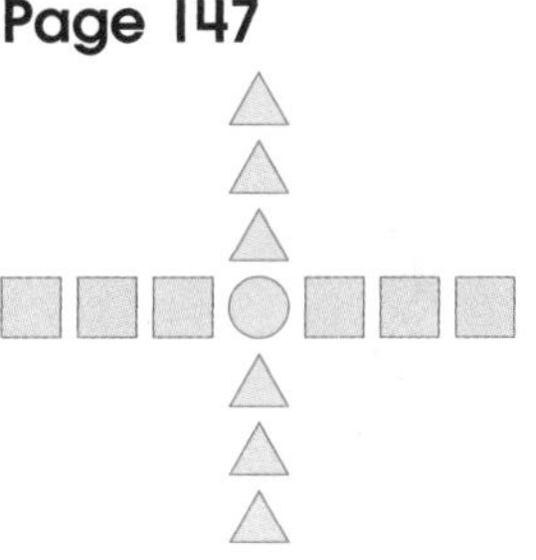

Page 148

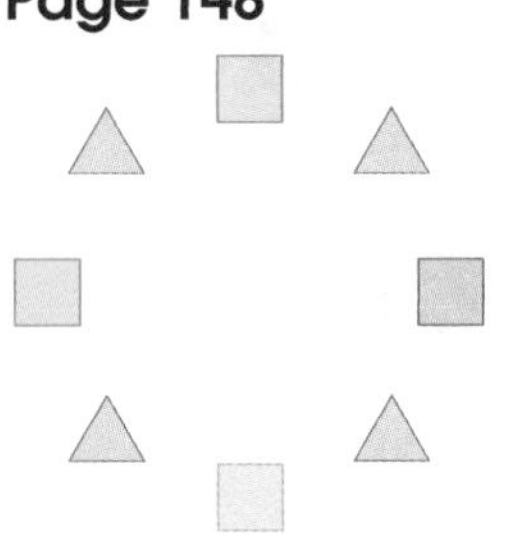

Page 149

Page 150
Pictures will vary.

Page 151
pound
foot
gallon

Page 152

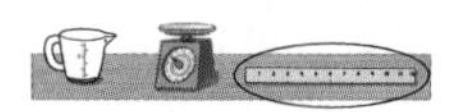

Page 153

Page 154
Pictures will vary.

Page 155

Page 156

Pictures will vary.

Page 157
years
inches
pounds

Page 158

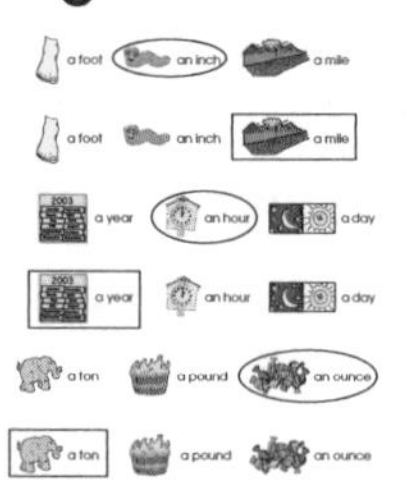

Page 159

Page 160

Page 161
both are round
one is flat and one is not
both are square
one is flat and one is not

Page 162
both have "points"
one is round and
one is square
both come in twos
both are different colors

Page 163

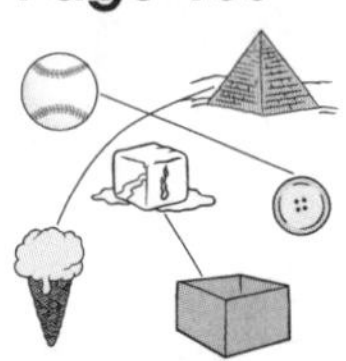

Page 164

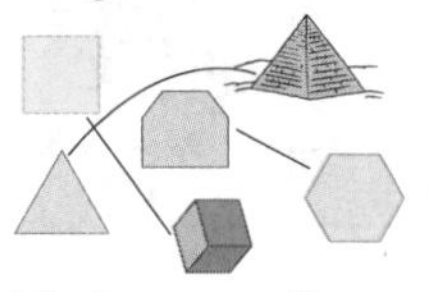

Pictures will vary.

Page 165

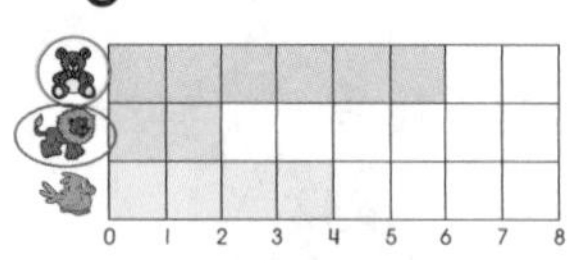

Answers will vary.

Page 166

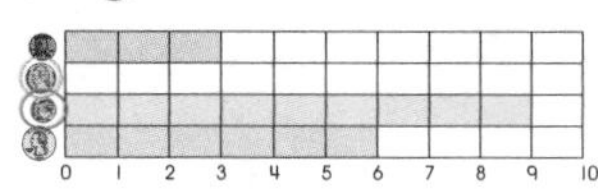

Answers will vary.

Page 167
10 ounces of juice
10 ounces of water

Page 168
6 ounces of juice
24 ounces of water

Page 169
10 shoes
3 hats
3 earmuffs

Page 170
16 shoes
5 hats
5 earmuffs

Page 171
3, 4, 8, 40

Page 172
3, 5, 10, 50

Page 173
3
7

Page 174
7
5

Page 175
13 circles
5 circles
10 circles
15 circles
5 circles

Page 176
15 circles
10 circles
10 circles
15 circles
5 circles

Page 177
6
5, 6, 7, and 8
5

Page 178
$4\frac{1}{2}$
-1, 0, 1, 2, and 3
$2\frac{1}{2}$

Page 179

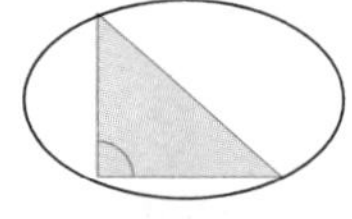

Pictures will vary.

Page 180

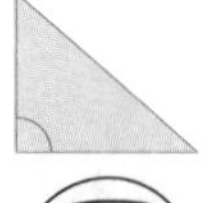
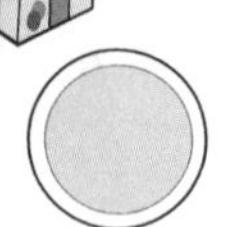
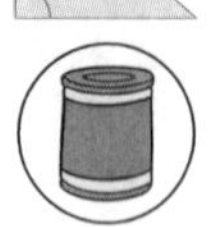

Pictures will vary.

Page 181
3 circles
6 colors
5 circles
Pictures will vary.

Page 182
2 circles
8 colors
3 circles

Notes

Notes

Notes